WITH A TAP ON THE KNEE

Memoirs of a Reluctant Banker

BOB RYAN

MIS BOOKS

Published in Ireland in 2001
by
MIS Books

ISBN 0 9541453 0 5

Jacket design by Orlagh Daly

Typeset in 11.5 point Times Roman with Bembo
by Alphabet Graphics, Dublin

Printed and bound by
Grafton Litho, Dublin

MIS BOOKS
P.O. Box 8250
Dun Laoghaire
Co. Dublin

For

Mary

John, Eamon, Robert and Marion

ACKNOWLEDGMENTS

This book would not have been possible without the support of a great many people.

First and foremost, I would like to thank my wife, Mary, for her constant encouragement of my efforts, which began in the autumn of 1997.

I am indebted to Mike Burns, who, having left a successful career in journalism and broadcasting to become a consultant in corporate and international affairs, took my manuscript and cast off bravely into the world of publishing, with his guiding light, his recently deceased wife, Lynette Fegen.

I am grateful to John Garvey of the Irish Press for reading an early draft of the manuscript and providing invaluable advice, and to my good friend, Michael Kennedy, who scrutinised the final version and offered many similarly useful comments.

Many thanks are due to friends and acquaintances from inside and outside of banking who helped to jog my memory and supplied comments, anecdotes, photographs and miscellaneous information. It is not possible to mention all of them here (some, indeed, have sadly passed away since this project began), but they include: Michael Cagney, Angela Cotter, Gerry Duff, Jim Fitzpatrick, Seamus Horgan, Con Howard, Niall Kerrigan, Tom Lawlor, Brian McCarthy, Ernie McElroy, Joe McGlinn, John Murphy, Niall Murphy, Margaret O'Dea, Paddy O'Grady Walshe, Gerry O'Mahony, Pat O'Mahony, John O'Shea, Brian Whelan and Jonathan Williams. My thanks also to AIB, the Irish Bank Officials Association, the Irish Times and the Irish Independent.

Finally, I would especially like to thank Emer Connolly, whose editing skills, patience and many hours of painstaking work greatly enhanced the original manuscript.

CONTENTS

1.	Opening Balance	1
2.	South Mall	8
3.	A Closer Inspection	19
4.	Among the Bolsheviks	29
5.	Body and Sole	36
6.	Cultural Capers	44
7.	T'ruppence Each de Starlights	54
8.	A Change of Direction	63
9.	Strike	70
10.	A Laundrette in London	77
11.	On Grub Street	87
12.	Pressing Concerns	93
13.	In Good Company	101
14.	Magic!	107
15.	Giants.	115
16.	Landmines	122
17.	In the Headlines	129
18.	Closing Statement	141

CHAPTER 1

OPENING BALANCE

Cork is a handsome city of limestone and red sandstone, its centre built on low marshy ground surrounded by hills. A grey and misty place when rain rolls in from the south-west, it acquires on sunny days a certain provincial elegance that only partly explains the unshakeable pride and confidence of its citizens.

I was born in Tramore in 1931, but it was in Cork that I spent the happiest of childhoods, in the rented house on the Victoria Road where I grew up with my brother and my five sisters. It was in Cork, too, that I first embarked on a career in banking, a profession often seen as synonymous with dullness which in my case somehow led me on to many adventures and provided me with enormous fun over the following four decades. Best of all, my years as a reluctant banker brought me into contact with a succession of memorable personalities, who became my companions, my influences and my friends. Their fingerprints are on my life, as mine may be on theirs.

During the years when I was growing up, my father, Innocent Ryan (known as Ino), was a bank inspector with the Munster & Leinster Bank; later he was transferred to Dublin, where he became manager of a branch in Crumlin. He was an interesting man with a great love of books and music (particularly choral music) and a wry sense of humour. His deeply held Christian faith combined orthodox Catholicism with surprisingly liberal views. I seldom heard him raise his voice in anger, which probably explains this comment of his, on his seven unruly offspring: 'One word from me and they do exactly what they like!'

My father was fond of relating stories and anecdotes, some of them perhaps apocryphal. One of his favourites described an incident which he said had taken place on the upper deck of a Cork bus, where he found himself sitting next to a well-heeled Montenotte matron. Disgusted by a small man in a cap repeatedly spitting on the floor, she enquired in a loud voice of the conductor, 'I say, is spitting allowed on this bus?' to which he airily replied, 'Spit away, ma'am, spit away!' My father would laugh heartily as he told us these stories.

My mother, Florence Carey, came from a seafaring family and grew up in Liverpool, although her ancestors on her father's side were Irish. She was a born actress, given to periodic displays of melodrama, but in spite of her stubbornly held opinions and judgments, she was an essentially gay, light-hearted woman who managed the family finances without too much thought for tomorrow. My mother shared my father's gregarious nature and love of music, and our home often rang to the sounds of organised parties and impromptu get-togethers, sometimes around the piano, where he would accompany her fine voice as they entertained friends and neighbours after a game of cards.

When I first set out to write this memoir (if the word is not too self-important), it was less out of any introspective autobiographical urge than from a desire to record an era in banking in Ireland which is now forever gone. Most of all, I wanted to commemorate some of the people I have known. It was not my intention to devote much space to the personal or to my own family background, but since I have an ancestor or two who strike me as of interest, I hope the reader will excuse a brief detour at this point.

As a child, my romantic imagination was captivated by stories of my two sailor uncles, my mother's brothers, and especially of her father, Captain William Carey, a sea-captain who perished in command of the SS *Vestris*, which met its doom on a Christmas voyage from New Jersey to Argentina in 1928. My introduction to the Internet in recent years has shed new light on this event, and has resulted in some interesting email correspondence from total strangers, including an American oceanographer who lost his grandparents and an uncle (then a child) in the disaster, and who appears to be well informed on maritime history.

The sinking of the *Vestris* was a sensational event at the time. Of the 326 people aboard, 112 died, and my email correspondent informs me that Captain Carey was 'severely handled' by the press. He himself believes that my grandfather was indeed partly responsible, but also that 'it was the system and command structure that was to blame, not just the Captains.' (He was referring here to both the *Vestris* and the *Titanic*.) He continues: 'They were, in my view, almost as much passive victims as the passengers. The book I referenced noted a change in British

Admiralty law as a result of findings dealing with undue corporate meddling (on the part of the shipping line) in the Captain's supposed authority.'

It struck me that this 'severe handling' of my grandfather by the press must have added to the trauma suffered by his family. My mother never spoke much about the circumstances of her father's death, and she took little interest, more than half a century later, when I excitedly showed her a photograph of the sinking of the ship which I had come across in an old book of photo-journalism discovered by accident in a Bed & Breakfast in Nenagh.

The Ryans appear to have been a very different breed. My grandfather, Bob Ryan (after whom I was named), had a brother named Innocent, who became Dean of Cashel. Noted for his trenchant views on matters of church and state, he seemed to preside over the family like some Roman general. He was reputed to have an equally formidable housekeeper who, the story goes, answered the bell one day to find an agitated delegation shuffling on the doorstep. 'Tell the Dane,' one of them drawled, 'that there's a gintleman here who'd like to have a word with him.' 'And which of you precisely,' she snapped back, 'is the *gintleman*?'

My granduncle was emphatically not an espouser of radical causes, and he adopted a strong anti-Sinn Féin stance during the War of Independence. So resolute was his opposition to De Valera that he once denounced one of the latter's speeches from the altar in Cashel. According to my grandfather's second wife (he remarried after my father's mother died), this so provoked the wrath of Sinn Féin that they arranged for a hired gunman to be brought in from a distant diocese and issued with the simple instruction to eliminate the Dean of Cashel. Unfortunately, he shot the Protestant Dean by mistake. When I tried to confirm this recently, I was told that it is one of the many fables that grew up around my austere and forthright granduncle during his long reign as Dean of Cashel, in itself an interesting reflection on the man. Perhaps at least some part of it is true.

The Ryans originated in the Glen of Aherlow in Co. Tipperary, where they were known as the Frewen Ryans. My father's name, Innocent, was a recurring first name in the family, a distinction which in my generation missed me to fall instead to my brother. (It has recently been conferred on one of my twin grandsons, the newest additions to the family.) I had always assumed that this unusual name was a throwback to the papacy, but research carried out by a cousin, Kay Frewen, along with her husband, Seamus Fleming, has revealed that the truth was probably very different.

It seems that the Frewens were Puritans who came to Ireland with Cromwell. Their family home in Northiam in Kent, still intact, is today a listed building. It was common practice among the Puritans to name their children after virtues (*Faith, Hope, Charity*), or – strangely to modern ears – using verb forms suggestive of worthy or desirable attributes, resulting in such curious first names as *Resolved.* The records show that the mostly Puritan passengers aboard the *Mayflower*, for example, included folk with names like *Desire, Love, Remembered* and *Humility*. One of the Frewen Ryans' more illustrious ancestors was *Accepted* Frewen, who held the rank of Archbishop of York in 1660. His brother's name was *Thankful*. The name *Innocent* is therefore almost certainly of Puritan origin, first appearing in Ireland with the marriage and issue of John Ryan and Mary Frewen of the Glen of Aherlow.

This, then, is a sample of my ancestry, the bloodline I inherited: sailors on the high seas on the one hand (a pirate or two would not surprise me); Puritans and archbishops on the other. It's as good an excuse as any!

~

My father would occasionally commit his thoughts to verse, and this short piece, composed one Christmas Eve after midnight Mass, probably expresses something of the philosophy on which his children were reared:

Alone with ham and stout
Nobody about
All money spent
Yet no repent
Hard though it came, what care?
It welcome went.

It was probably not my parents' intention that this seemingly carefree attitude to life should sit so comfortably with the natural inclinations of their first-born. By the time I was ten, it was obvious that I was a dreamer, drawn magnetically to other dreamers and to the local ne'er-do-wells. My mother in particular viewed my choice of friends with alarm. I was fatally attracted to the kind of schoolboy daring and high spirits that rarely go hand-in-hand with discipline or a serious attitude to schoolwork. My career as a boy scout lasted all of two days.

Despite the best efforts of the Presentation Brothers, it was clear by the time I had reached my mid-teens that I was not headed for a promising academic career. A family conference was held and the various options laid out. There was a feeling that I would never acquire the *gravitas* appropriate to a civil servant, while a mention of insurance from someone drew the scathing comment: 'guaranteed to insure the lamest duck!' The church – the dream of so many Irish mothers for their sons – was never mentioned, for I had failed to make the grade even as an altar boy. Since early childhood I had always loved to draw and paint (I was also attracted to music), but in the mid-1940s, none of this was taken very seriously. They may have been acceptable leisure interests, but I doubt if it ever crossed anybody's mind – perhaps least of all my own – to look to them for any clue as to how a young man might go about earning a living. The pressure was on to acquire a respectable, permanent position, and the choices were limited.

The discussion ended inconclusively, and I returned to my daydreams of swaggering up Patrick Street (an activity known in Cork as 'doing Pana') as an international football star, giving the once-over to the perambulating talent and bestowing a wink on someone special who might catch my eye. I imagined myself deafening the residents of Victoria Road as I hit top gear as a champion racing motor-cyclist, or soaring over Montenotte as a daring Spitfire pilot to gasps of admiration from small boys.

This Walter Mitty-like existence ended abruptly some weeks later when my father approached me to announce that he had succeeded in obtaining what was known as a 'nomination' for me in the Munster & Leinster Bank. Following in one's father's footsteps was very much a feature of both the skilled trades and the professions at the time, but I had somehow not seen myself in the role of banker. What would my lawless friends say?

My mother began to petition assorted saints, including one in charge of lost causes. She was seriously concerned that without concerted human and divine intervention, I might end up joining the local corner-boys, whose backsides held up the courthouse on Washington Street. The Brothers had a special class for bank entrants, and I was quickly enrolled. Six months later I had crammed enough into my still-reeling brain to get through a special examination for the sons of bank officials. The freedom of my happy summer days down the Boggy Road was already receding into memory.

~

In 1913, the people of Cork came out to gaze with pride on a new building that had been erected for the Munster & Leinster Bank at 66 South Mall. Joining in the chorus of praise, the Cork Examiner in its issue of 14 June described it thus:

> *'a practical scheme of offices, and exceedingly rich interior decorations. The Dome of the Banking Hall is supported on monolith marble columns from the celebrated quarries of Spezzia, beautiful red, wonderfully streaked and waved. Six of these pillars were once intended to be erected to carry the organ in the south transept of St. Paul's Cathedral. As the design of the Architect, Mr. Arthur Hill, provided for eight monoliths, the quarry at Spezzia had to be re-opened to provide material for the requisite number, which now gives such grandeur to the Hall.'*

Cork would have expected nothing less. Its familiarity with the world of banking went back a long way. In 1296, the title of Sheriff of Cork was held by Cambinus Donati of Florence, one of a number of Italian merchant bankers then plying their trade in northern Europe. After the coming of the Normans, Edward I of England had despatched Donati and others to act as bailiffs, bankers and revenue collectors in Ireland. The Florentine's position suggests that Cork was already of some importance in the thirteenth century, one of the first cities in Ireland to become involved in what passed for banking at the time.

Such useful titbits of information were wholly absent from my mind as I presented myself for interview to the board of the Munster & Leinster Bank at 66 South Mall. Scrubbed, brushed and uncomfortable in my suit, I waited for some time in an oak-panelled office before being ushered into the boardroom. I took a seat and nervously faced the ancient, sober gentlemen assembled at the other end of a long table, some of them slumped in leather chairs and looking slightly drowsy. Unnerving intervals seemed to elapse between questions.

'So, eh, what games do you play, then?'

'A bit of everything…sir.'

'Tennis?'

'Well, no.'

'Golf, maybe?'

'Eh, no, sir – not golf.'

A long pause. 'I see.'

Eventually, we got around to: 'And would you plan on staying with the bank, should we offer you a position?' This was clearly a key question. I offered a straight bat, injecting my response with as much false enthusiasm as I could muster.

'Oh, yes, sir!'

'Thank you, Ryan. You may leave.'

I had been called by my surname for the first time.

Strolling down Patrick Street afterwards, I was troubled by a feeling that it had all seemed too easy, although I don't know what else I might have expected, since my nomination and examination results were already fair indication that my fate was sealed.

And so it proved. Some weeks later a letter arrived offering me a position, subject to a medical examination, which I assumed to be designed to give me a thorough physical check-out. In the event, it turned out to be a perfunctory affair.

'Open your mouth,' the doctor barked. 'Say "Aaah".'

'Aaaaaah.'

'Now, sit up there and let your leg hang loose.'

A tap on the knee with a rubber mallet, and I was on my way to a career in the bank.

CHAPTER 2

SOUTH MALL

The Banking Hall of the Munster & Leinster Bank at 66 South Mall was built to impress, to give comfort and confidence to those who entrusted their wealth to the prudent, worthy and far-seeing gentlemen who made up the banking fraternity. When I joined the bank in 1949, my first impressions were of highly polished mahogany counters, palms in brass containers, walls painted a dull green and a fine glass dome. A quiet hush prevailed, broken only by the sound of a typewriter and a low murmur of voices. Overhead, on a marble-floored balcony with wrought-iron balustrade, senior bankers could sometimes be seen pacing to and fro with the merchant princes, the captains of Cork's industry, pausing from time to time to gaze down thoughtfully on their loyal customers and staff. Head Office conducted its affairs on the upper storeys; the public office was confined to the ground floor.

Dress code was strict: dark suits, white collar, tie. A sports jacket was permitted – on Saturdays. The wearer might be going on to an afternoon of fishing or golf: the bank understood such things. Haircuts were uniform: short back and sides. Beards were strictly forbidden.

I soon got to know my fellow-workers, who came in a surprising variety of shapes and sizes. There were tall, skinny men who gobbled like nervous turkeys; small chaps with inflated undercarriages who wheezed a lot and grumbled under their breath; one or two ascetics who might have come straight from the parsonage; and an abundance of country lads from the farmlands of Munster. The staff was largely male, the feminine gender represented by just a handful of lively young women and a few mature ladies, all clad in the same navy-blue office coats with white collars, under the watchful eye of a sophisticated-looking supervisor whose official title was 'The Lady Superintendent'. The manager was addressed at all times as 'Manager': 'Yes, Manager,'; 'No, Manager,'; 'I'll see to that right away, Manager.'

Gradually I came to realise that this physical diversity reflected a kaleidoscope of personalities lurking behind standard haircuts and pen-pushing hands. Square pegs abounded, free spirits corralled unwillingly by the harsh economic climate and rigid social conventions of the time. One who fell into this category (although it would be some years later before I encountered him) was the painter, Tony O'Malley, who once told me that these banking misfits reminded him of seagulls clinging to rocks in severe winter storms. Few families could afford to provide a university education, and like teaching and the civil service, banking offered a well-regarded career.

Before applying for a position, however, one had first to be 'nominated' by someone the bank respected, feared, wished to cultivate or was indebted to in some way. Out of this system came a remarkable cross-section of individuals, some of whom, like Tony O'Malley, later succeeded in escaping and reinventing themselves at pursuits more suited to their temperaments. Perhaps following the lead given by the nineteenth-century poet, William Allingham, they included, down through the years, writers like Paddy Boyle and Frank Harvey; the artist, Cecil Galbally; T. P. McKenna, the actor; cartoonist, Paddy Ambrose; the popular singer and songwriter, Christy Moore; Formula One racing supremo, Eddie Jordan; and a variety of TV and radio personalities such as Terry Wogan, Andy O'Mahony, Bunny Carr and Frank Delaney. Many others – potential poets, sculptors, dramatists and philosophers (or, for that matter, surgeons, bishops, entrepreneurs, athletes and even gardeners) stayed forever imprisoned behind bank counters, but while they lived out their lives with their eyes apparently fixed on their ledgers, their souls remained gloriously elsewhere. They added a dimension of colour to our otherwise dull days in the bank, and were a link with the heart of the country.

The first of this species to cross my path was John Mansfield from Cobh, fifteen miles down the railway track from Cork. A lean man in his forties, he sat on a tall stool at a pock-marked table in a corner of the office, sorting cheques. Unruly grey wispy hair topped a gaunt ascetic face, and a frayed tweed suit hung loosely over his bony frame. Finance – national, corporate or even personal – was not one of John's interests. He lived in a rented house and rode a rusty bicycle; his possessions were few. Every morning he shuffled his frail, rather bent figure into the office and climbed on to his stool, mind swarming with ideas on history, philosophy and literature. His head would remain bent over his work for a long time; then, suddenly throwing an arm skywards, he would excitedly declaim, 'Plato and Aquinas – that's the link!'

John had a long-suffering assistant, a middle-aged woman named Mary Moynihan, who would stand respectfully by, awaiting his instructions on the ever-mounting batches of cheques that needed to be sorted and dispatched to the various banks. Stretching a skinny arm towards her, John would intone:

'This is the hour that we must mourn,
With tallow on the black triangle.'

A look of dread would descend upon Mary's face. 'What's that, Mr. Mansfield?' she would ask nervously.

'Austin Clarke, Mary – *Tenebrae*.' Leaning back, he would tilt his face to the heavens, eyes closed. 'Do you ever think of the day, Mary, when you will be laid out on a slab of cold marble?'

'Oh, Mr. Mansfield – please,' his assistant would moan.

But John would be off, unable to stop himself:

'The agony of the man betrayed
At every station of the cross!'

'Will I start totting up the cheques now, Mr. Mansfield?'

Above all, Mansfield was a visionary, given to pursuing lofty but hopelessly impractical and unattainable ideals. Despite his unmaterialistic nature, he sometimes allowed himself to be tempted into strange enterprises. He once bought a secondhand telephone kiosk, probably because it seemed too good a bargain to miss. On another occasion, after overhearing some discussion on the bright future of the poultry industry, he appeared in the office carrying a large cardboard box with air holes cut in the sides, from which came the unmistakable sound of the chirping of day-old chicks. He had decided that the future lay in intensive battery rearing, and had acquired a hundred birds which he intended to raise under a bulb in his spare room. Alas, John's compassionate nature got the better of him, and one fine sunny day when it was a joy to be outdoors, he let his birds out for some fresh air. He had forgotten that their wings were not clipped, and soon he was to be seen tearing up and down the streets of Cobh, clutching a sack, his old hobnailed army boots knocking sparks off the cobblestones as he flung himself into gardens and through the open doors of houses in pursuit of his ungrateful flock.

It was probably his attachment to moral principles that had led Mansfield to become a soldier. At the outbreak of the Second World War, the banks released staff who wished to sign up with the army. It was assumed they would become commissioned officers, and the banks agreed to make up any shortfall between their bank and army earnings. This was less generous than it might at first appear, since those concerned were generally paid little in the bank and only slightly less in the army – perhaps a shilling or two a week.

John Mansfield applied to join the Construction Corps, probably out of some vague interest in architecture or engineering. It turned out to be one of the toughest squads in the army: a heavy-duty outfit composed mainly of hardy men with calloused hands and ox-like strength, who, as hod-carriers and human cement mixers, had tunnelled under Britain and built her roads, bridges, hospitals and schools. Many of them had decided that if they were going to have to spend time soldiering, it might as well be in the Free State army. And so, shorn of hair, and all skin and bone, Mansfield the philosopher took his place among the raw-boned campaigners of Camden, Dagenham and Cricklewood. He had been designated corporal, but his military career was doomed to failure, for if there was one thing that caused John serious distress, it was the misuse of language. Standing to attention with his unit one morning before an ill-tempered, roaring drill sergeant, he could not resist turning round to remonstrate with a foul-mouthed trooper whispering behind him. Stripped of his corporal's rank, he spent the next week peeling potatoes. He was reinstated, but within weeks the incident was repeated. He suffered great torments from his comrades, the navvies of the Construction Corps. Once, gazing up at the tricolour flying over the barracks, he was heard to mutter with a sigh, 'All this for Ireland!'

John returned to civilian life as a bank official in Buttevant, Co. Cork. One of the few customers of any importance in this branch was a wealthy, cantankerous old lady who sported a wispy beard on a stubborn chin. One morning she swept into the bank ready for combat, only to be confronted by the sight of John behind the counter, razor in hand and a lather of foam on his face, humming cheerfully as his thoughts roved pleasantly. Momentarily stunned into silence, she paused to stare. As if sensing a presence, John glanced around. Suddenly awoken from his reverie, he interrupted his task to boom jovially at her, 'Next for shaving?'

At 66 South Mall, the day inevitably came when Mary Moynihan reached the limit of her endurance. One afternoon, she burst into the assistant manager's office in a state of distress.

'Mr. Canty!' she cried, 'I can't take this any more! Please can I have another job!'

Pat Canty sighed. 'What is it this time, Miss Moynihan?'

'It's Mr. Mansfield!'

'What's he up to now?'

'He's walking around in his bare feet!'

Canty, a barrel of a man and a formidable prop-forward with Cork Constitution, strode out to investigate. Glaring pointedly at the unshod feet, he poked Mansfield in the ribs with a large forefinger and growled at him,' What's the idea, John? You can't walk around the bank like that. What are you at, at all?'

'Sorry, Pat,' replied John, affably. 'Just hardening up the feet, you know.'

'Hardening up…? For what, man?'

'Lough Derg, of course! I will be undertaking a penitential exercise in Lough Derg next week, Pat. I'm preparing the feet in advance.'

The assistant manager looked Mansfield in the eye. 'John,' he declared, 'we already have one poor sufferer doing penance in here – and that's Mary Moynihan. Get your boots back on this minute or you can stay permanently in Lough Derg!'

As he wandered past me in search of his footwear, I could hear John murmur sadly, 'What this country needs is *vision!*'

~

The lower orders on the ground floor were always alert to the movements of the powerful elements above us who were masterminding the affairs of the bank. We always moved aside to let our betters pass, and we were careful never to be observed idle. Like the rabbit with the fox, we kept a wary eye.

Some of those on the upper floor had genuine ability; others were said to have elbowed their way into positions of influence and responsibility. The seriousness of their task could be seen in their demeanour. They wore better-cut suits and inscrutable expressions. They seldom socialised with the run-of-the-mill humanity labouring below them, although on suitable occasions, they might permit us to see that in spite of the gravity and importance of their work, they were, after all, only flesh and blood. Their occasional forays into our world were never overdone, however, and rarely went beyond a drink to mark the festive season or a transfer.

Career paths were followed with intense interest. Was this a move up, down or sideways? With every new appointment, there were always those watching from the wings who would intimate that they 'knew it all along', who were expert at adjusting their footwork to accommodate the new power shifts, smug when they found that they had backed a winner.

The bank's customers, too, were affected by the atmosphere of the office. They were generally respectful – if not fearful – in approaching the counter. At that time, to open a current account in a bank one needed an introduction from someone of standing in the community. If anything was presented slightly out of order, the applicant was given short shrift.

The human face of the bank manifested itself principally in the porters. Johnny Spillane, the head porter at 66 South Mall, was a former sergeant in the Munster Fusiliers who had spent the greater part of the First World War in a German prison camp. Although short in stature, Johnny was every inch a soldier in his green porter's uniform, polished black boots and back straight as a ramrod. As important customers entered or left the bank, he would open the door, salute and click his heels. One day, the manager at South Mall, Tom Casey, was puzzled to notice that Johnny had failed to perform this drill with a customer generally regarded as being a person of some consequence.

'Johnny,' he enquired, 'wasn't Colonel Smyth in the Munster Fusiliers with you?'

'He was, sir.'

'He was a prisoner of war, like yourself?'

'He was indeed, sir.'

'I notice you didn't open the door for him – a fellow Fusilier and a prisoner of war?'

Johnny's lips came together in a disapproving line. He hesitated for a second before leaning towards the manager to spit contemptuously out of the corner of his mouth: 'Taken carrying his blankets, sir!'

'Carrying his…?'

'Went over to the Germans, sir! Blankets under the arm!'

As far as Johnny was concerned, the Colonel had disgraced himself and was unworthy of full military honours.

The porter who manned the upper floor, Gerry O'Callaghan, was another formidable figure, well over six feet tall. He too was a war veteran. Although now retired from his post as a sergeant in the Irish Guards, he remained forever on sentry duty, with the onerous task of guarding the premises of the bank's Head Office. No one passed through without his clearance. Gerry was an avid follower of Dolphin Rugby Club, and in moments of high excitement he was sometimes moved to express his support in military terms.

'Steady, boys! Fixed bayonets! Up and over!'

'Six inches of cold steel – that'll put the fear of God in them!'

The players must have been bewildered by the words, but there was no doubting the sentiment behind them.

Apart from the porters, the staff at South Mall also included a few other ex-soldiers, some of whom had managed to retain their army titles, along with a tendency to issue even the most mundane instructions in the form of barked commands. Many of them had been members of the Irish defence forces during the Emergency, and their experience introduced a note of unexpected militancy to the banking community, particularly within the union – the Irish Bank Officials' Association – which I was invited to join within days of entering the bank.

The ink on my application form was scarcely dry, when, on Christmas Eve 1950, Michael Corish, representing the union, stood on a table and announced an all-out strike for increased salaries and better conditions of employment. There was consternation. The militants rubbed their hands and slapped each other on the back. Others shook their heads and declared that no good could come of it. A few averted their eyes and looked uneasy, unsure of which way to turn, while the gobbling of the turkeys rose several octaves. As for me, I stood firm with the majority of the younger staff and new recruits, whose eyes shone in joyful anticipation of something – anything – happening. Barely in the door and we were already on strike: things were looking up! We were taken under the wings of the warriors, who made belligerent noises and lost no time in heading for Davy Mac's licensed premises to celebrate Christmas and discuss a plan of action.

The strike lasted for seven weeks. The countryside that winter was dusted by a sprinkling of snow, and it was particularly cold.

Picketing a branch was described as 'observing', which meant keeping a watching brief from a discreet distance. Some confined their 'observation' duties to installing themselves in the comfort of a convenient nearby pub window, armed against the inclement weather with hot whiskeys.

My father was a senior inspector in the bank, and although a member of the IBOA, he was what was known as an 'exempt official', which meant that he was permitted by the union to continue working during the strike. One afternoon, as I was dutifully 'observing' through the window of Davy Mac's, a car and a container van drew up and entered the side gate of the bank. I saw my father step out from behind the wheel of the car. I knew about his exempt status, but I was curious about the van and its contents. It was only many years later, however, that I succeeded in pressing him on this incident. He told me that he had been supervising the delivery of a consignment of gold from the Vatican, which was being despatched for safe-keeping to the vaults of the bank. The Cold War was then at its height, and the Vatican had become concerned at the political turbulence in Italy. There was a view that if a communist government took over, it would lead inexorably towards the creation of a Soviet-controlled Italian state. As a result, the Vatican had decided to transfer some of its assets from Italian financial institutions to safer foreign banks. I remember being surprised and vaguely impressed that the Munster & Leinster should be among the chosen. At the time when all of this was happening, however, my father's only response to my enquiries was a dry, 'And *where* exactly did you say you were you watching from?'

The strike ended and the humdrum routine of work resumed. As my handwriting – the only skill for which I had ever won a prize at school – was considered legible, I found myself charged with responsibility for writing deposit receipts. I quickly mastered this intricate art, having absorbed the one vital instruction given to me: 'Only write exactly what's in front of you. If it says "Dan Barry", don't, for God's sake, put down "Daniel Barry" instead.'

New friends and the increasing recruitment of female staff put a fresh spring in my step, relieving the boredom of the job. Amorous attachments came and went. If you were spotted going to the pictures with the same girl twice, the word would spread: 'They're doing a line!' A few more sightings and marriage might even be mentioned – although on a salary of twelve pounds a month, it was hardly likely.

The search for romance was never-ending: in winter in smoky dance-halls; in summer on day-trips by bus to places like Sherkin Island off Baltimore. These outings were eagerly anticipated (not least because they were popular with the girls), but they somehow never quite fulfilled their promise. Instead, my friends and I would end up downing pints of stout in a pub, while the girls who had accompanied us went swimming or sightseeing, unimpressed by demonstrations of male camaraderie and the raucous singing of ballads like *The Banks* or *The Bould Thady Quill*. The chorus would reach new heights on the return journey, although by then some were usually reduced to snoring at the back of the bus, while the women huddled together for safety at the front.

In truth, when it came to the opposite sex, the gap between our aspirations and our *savoir faire* was the source of constant disappointment. My own head was hopelessly turned by the cinema starlets of the day, and I envied the sophistication of the men who wooed them. Going to the pictures was a favourite occupation. I remember queuing in great excitement outside the *Ritz* to see what was reputed to be a daring continental film, *Bitter Rice*, which had somehow escaped the censor's normally vigilant scissors. It starred a sultry Italian actress, Silvana Mangano, who seemed to spend much of her time on-screen wading through rice fields with her skirts tucked up, exposing sensual thighs. This was heady stuff, and it drove the testosterone levels of the men of Cork dangerously high. Under the influence of the film and the seductive performance of Mangano, I fell captive to Italian beauty and embarked on a series of fantasy love affairs with the likes of Sophia Loren and Claudia Cardinale. The English and American stars of the day seemed like brittle porcelain in comparison.

At home, apart from the *Cork Examiner* and the *Irish Times*, there was a reasonably good selection of books at our disposal. The classics were well represented, along with biographies of important figures in world history and politics. My father was also a regular subscriber to the *New Statesman*, and I recall him recommending it to me as a superbly written periodical on international affairs. It was only much later that I discovered how radical its left-wing stance was for the times, particularly in Ireland.

With plenty of spare time, no money and no steady 'line' to occupy me, painting became my outlet. I applied to the Crawford School of Art for admission to night classes and discovered a way to give shape to my dreams. By day, as I scratched away on my hundred-thousandth deposit receipt with my steel N-Nib, my mind would stray a million miles away as I made plans to follow in the footsteps of the French painter, Paul Gauguin. I saw myself living on a tropical island surrounded by olive-skinned maidens, lolling in warm seas, feasting on exotic fruits and painting to my heart's content, while birds of paradise circled slowly in blue skies overhead.

One day as I was engrossed in these sustaining reveries, a dark shadow fell over my desk. It was Mr. Blake from the Branch Department. His stern face and merciless eye fixed on my meandering hand as it traced its leisurely path across yet another deposit receipt.

'Ryan! What's that you're using?'

'P...pardon, Mr. Blake?'

'What ink is that you're using?'

'It's...Quink, Mr. Blake,' I said weakly, indicating the label, confused by a sense of guilt but having no idea what I had done.

'Precisely! Let me draw your attention to that ink, Ryan. Do you not know that Quink ink is washable?'

'Washable?'

'Yes, washable! That means that it can be rubbed out easily. Where is the bank's black ink, Ryan?'

'I thought...blue...might look better on the receipts.'

There was a loud intake of breath as Blake drew his shoulders back, quivered slightly and glared down at me from his full height. 'Ryan,' he barked, 'there is one thing you must always remember in the bank. *You are not paid to think!*' With that, and to demonstrate beyond doubt the ink's inferior qualities, he took one of my completed deposit receipts, licked his enormous thumb and started to rub vigorously. Within seconds, he had rubbed a hole in the receipt.

'There!' he declared. 'What did I tell you!'

~

Had Mr. Blake only realised it, the question of ink was about to become irrelevant, for it was around this time that the ballpoint pen arrived, provoking serious debate as to whether it constituted a proper, legal pen, suitable for the bank's activities. In my mind's eye, I imagined Blake conducting tests, his outsized thumb working overtime in an effort to gauge its indelible qualities. The old leather-bound ledgers had always been written in careful copperplate handwriting, naturally using the bank's indelible ink and the trusty steel N-Nib. It was said that the biro would ruin good handwriting, but already rumour had it that two biros were being kept under lock and key in Head Office. The days when a man could earn his living by the quality of his handwriting were numbered. It was the end of the era of the N-Nib. I looked at the welt on my finger, and hoped it was true.

The demise of pen and ink also implied a farewell to blotting paper, with which bank clerks were well supplied for drying the wet ink on cheques, receipts and official documents. The ordained procedure was that one laid the receipt on the blotting paper – never the other way around. Fresh sheets of white blotting paper were placed on the bank counters every morning for the convenience of the public.

Also set to vanish forever were the days when men in spectacles could glance down long columns of figures and insert correct totals. Already, people were gathering around to admire the totting machine, the first manifestation of the new, advanced office machinery (the word technology had yet to gain currency), and as far as I was concerned, it too had arrived not a moment too soon. It was followed by the 'waste machine', a curious name for a grey contraption with a keyboard, banked on all sides by metal pigeonholes for the cheques being processed. An invitation to take control of this mammoth suggested that your career was headed in the right direction.

The clanking of these new wonder machines soon became a familiar sound, reminding us of the dynamism and progressive nature of the bank – never mind that some branches had yet to install a telephone. Change was in the air, and people began to move to its rhythm. The monarchs of the upper floor strode the balcony ever more frequently, fretting over these expensive toys and anxious for reassurance that their minions were adapting. Below, those who had previously taken minutes to get from one end of the office to the other could now be seen striding purposefully about, wearing serious faces and waving long rolls of paper which streamed out behind them as they passed. A new sense of opportunity hovered about the banking hall. To some at least, the future whispered seductively.

CHAPTER 3

A CLOSER INSPECTION

The culture of banking in Ireland has changed so dramatically over the past few decades that the present generation of bankers could scarcely even imagine the world in which I found myself when I joined the Munster & Leinster Bank a few years after the end of the War. Until well into the 1960s, bank officials were a rootless community, subject to transfer at the whim of Head Office. Your one certainty upon joining the bank was that you would never find yourself working within twenty miles of your home town, insider knowledge being considered risky.

Very few bank staff had cars, and fewer still owned their own houses. Bank managers and their wives were expected to deal in shops and businesses which kept their accounts with the bank. This could mean that the manager's wife might find herself buying her meat from the inferior butcher at the far end of the town rather than from the man across the street with a reputation for the excellence of his prime beef. Sons and daughters of bankers who, like me, also went into the bank, were generally based in the branch where their father worked.

The only local employed by the bank was the porter, and the porter's position was thus in many ways an important one. My friend, Jack Ringrose, once told me that his first step on being appointed branch manager in a town in Co. Limerick was to make friends with the porter. He shrewdly realised that it would take him years to acquire the man's knowledge and familiarity with the customers. They came to an arrangement whereby the porter would vigorously rub his nose to warn him of the approach of a customer who might need watching, while a scratch of the ear indicated an 'all clear'.

The staffs of the various banks mixed easily, bonded by their common status as 'blow-ins' and knowing, as they did, that they would never be fully accepted as locals. They all worked in similar conditions; their salary scales were identical, and they all feared the dreaded letter from Head Office informing them that they were to report within the month to a branch in some one-pub town in the remotest corner of Ireland.

Although lending money was the backbone of the industry, banks did not always look kindly on staff applying for a loan. During my early years in the bank, the very idea of applying for a house loan, for example, would fill a young banker with fear. In fact, with few exceptions, a mortgage was out of the question up until the late 1950s, and for years thereafter was given only grudgingly. To borrow money suggested that your finances were out of control – you were one to be watched.

Unauthorised 'loans' were dealt with ruthlessly. To be caught taking even the smallest amount from the till was to warrant instant dismissal. Those who had an interest in horse-racing or enjoyed a flutter on a dog were very vulnerable, and the temptation to borrow a pound note to put on a hotly-tipped horse could be hard to resist. The animal's failure to oblige would then lead to further temptation to 'borrow' again in an attempt to recover the situation. More people lost their job in the bank over losses incurred in the bookie's office than for any other reason.

Every evening, cashiers had to balance to the last penny the cash for which they were responsible. Any excess was held in a special account pending the possibility of a customer's claim on it; any shortfall had to made up from the cashier's own pocket. If a substantial amount went missing and the cashier was unable either to trace the shortage or replace the money, the branch manager would write to Head Office outlining the circumstances of the loss: '*We beg to advise that cashier, Jeremiah O'Riordan, notwithstanding a diligent search, has failed to trace...*' From Head Office would come the reproving response: '*We are dismayed to learn...*' A loan would generally be arranged, which the unfortunate cashier would have to pay back over time.

This careful choice of words was a feature of every written communication issued by the bank. Eschewing creativity in favour of a style whose only concern was that no word or phrase should ever be open to a misinterpretation (particularly one that might one day work to the bank's disadvantage), banks churned out correspondence that was often barely comprehensible to the ordinary citizen. Branch managers were encouraged to adopt this style in communicating both with customers and with Head Office, while Head Office in turn carefully measured every word despatched to the branches. A manager was generally addressed as *Dear Sir*, but at 66 South Mall and at Dame Street branch in Dublin, he was deemed worthy of *My Dear Sir*. And lest a manager might feel he had some proprietary right to the branch, his internal correspondence was always addressed to the 'Manager *at*' and never to the 'Manager *of*' that branch.

Some managers never quite conformed to the Head Office style. One, perhaps a minimalist by nature, or in rebellion at the dominant bureaucracy, found his own formula for dealing with customers who had become overdrawn. His letters ran along these lines:

Dear Mr. Brown,
Lodge.
Yours sincerely,
James Mullarkey.
Manager.

Such clarity of expression had its virtues. It entirely escaped another, newly transferred manager, who arrived in the town that was to be his new home only to find that his predecessor had removed almost everything from the living quarters provided above the bank, including the bathroom mirror. His letter to Head Office detailing his needs included a request for permission for '*a permanent erection in the bathroom.*'

Much of the branches' correspondence with Head Office began: *I beg to advise*, or *I beg permission.* The word 'appear' was much favoured: '*we do not appear to have received...*' or '*there appears to be some difficulty...*' The problem of selecting the appropriate language could sometimes be avoided altogether by using a handy pre-printed memorandum supplied by the bank, which allowed the manager to fill in the blanks as appropriate. It usually began: '*I*, (manager's name and branch address, pre-printed) *wish to report...*' The manager's name appeared again at the end, requiring only a scrawled signature above it.

One story is told of a branch manager who went fishing one summer's evening and, while trying to land a large fish, slipped, fell into the river and drowned. Like many others at the time, the branch did not have a telephone, and the nervous recently appointed assistant manager knew that he must report the tragic news to Head Office. Perhaps he wished to do this with greater delicacy than would have been possible in a telegram, for one of his deceased manager's pre-printed memos soon reached Dublin bearing a report that went something like this:

I, John Smith of Carrickoshaughlin branch, wish to report...(here he conscientiously inserted various matters of routine information relating to balances of accounts, loans outstanding, and the like).

Finally, I wish to report that yesterday, 6th July, having finished my day's work at 5.00 p.m., I checked that the cash had balanced, locked the vault and went fishing on the Annagarry river. Unfortunately, I lost my footing, fell in and was drowned. Due to this unfortunate accident, I have been unable to resume duty at the branch, where my assistant manager, T. H. Sweeney, has replaced me pending further instructions.

Yours truly,
John Smith,
Manager.

If discretion was strongly advocated in documents emanating from within the bank, even greater care was recommended in the scrutiny of anything issuing from outside the bank that might require a response on the bank's part. Managers in particular sometimes needed a lawyer's instinct for the meaning behind words in order to protect the bank's interest and avoid taking imprudent action. Their role also called for much common sense. Some displayed little of either.

A manager once received a letter from a well-to-do customer seeking his assistance in making an investment,'as per enclosed'. The 'enclosed' turned out to be a newspaper cutting advertising a greyhound for sale. The manager was a little surprised, but was willing to act as intermediary. He arranged a meeting between the man and the advertiser at the bank.

The two duly presented themselves, and after a few words of introduction, got down to business. The prospective buyer opened negotiations by announcing that he was not going to beat about the bush: he would make a first and final offer of £3,000, and the vendor could take it or leave it. If the owner of the dog looked surprised, the bank manager was stunned. The vendor eventually found his voice, muttered that the offer was a generous one and declared his intention to accept. Not wishing to sound too eager, he hastily added that he did of course realise that the bitch was guaranteed to produce a winner when mated with the right animal. The purchaser followed this with some bewilderment. 'Greyhound?' he interrupted, 'What greyhound? What in the name of God are you talking about?' At that moment, the manager's eye lit upon the newspaper cutting on his desk. By chance, it was lying the wrong way up. On the reverse he read a heading in large letters: *Investment Property For Sale.*

~

Next to an unwelcome transfer, the greatest fear of bank officials everywhere was a visit from an inspector. Now replaced by soft-focus auditors who arrive at a branch breathing concern and good-will ('We're here to help…'), bank inspectors struck terror in the hearts of the banking fraternity up and down the country. Their visits were regarded as a sort of Judgment Day. Every transaction since the last visit was gone through with a fine-comb: there could be no hiding place. Such was the level of fear that a trembling bank official might even attempt to end his agony by confessing in advance to some minor misdeed.

Apart from conducting the audit, inspectors (known as 'Beaks') also reported on the conduct of the manager and staff of the branch. This had the effect of inducing a rapid tidy-up whenever an inspection seemed imminent. The usual bottles of stale milk and curling sandwiches disappeared from desktops. Cardigans normally worn under suits were stuffed into drawers; shoes were polished on the backs of trouser legs. It was deemed inadvisable to be seen smoking during public hours, and lunchtimes became teetotal, as no one would have dared run the risk of creating even the slightest trace of alcohol fumes.

The inspector would also generally take a look around to see whether the manager's dining room required a new coat of paint or the roof was short of a few slates. Even the manager's wife was scrutinised: she was expected to be a model of propriety in the community, not given to idle gossiping or other inappropriate behaviour.

Any serious misdemeanour uncovered by an inspection was generally taken for adjudication to a higher authority, which alone was empowered to pronounce judgment and dish out penance – usually a transfer to a crossroads branch in the middle of a bog. Very occasionally, someone might disappear altogether, never to be heard of again. When an inspector had completed his inspection and departed, he left behind him a branch shorn of bad habits, where the petty cash and stamp accounts balanced to the last penny every evening and no transaction was undertaken that did not follow the precise procedures ordained for it from on high. This state of affairs often lasted for as long as three weeks.

Bank inspections gave rise to many stories. One that circulated widely concerned a Bank of Ireland branch in a small town in the West of Ireland, where an inspector arrived one afternoon to find the doors open but no one behind the counter. A murmur of voices came from the manager's room, where the staff were engrossed in a game of cards. The inspector pressed the alarm button. At first, nothing happened. Then brisk footsteps were heard approaching outside, and a man in an apron appeared bearing a tray heavy with pints of stout. He was fulfilling his part in a long-standing arrangement between the bank and the publican across the street, whereby the sound of the alarm signalled a need for refreshments.

There were a number of bank inspectors whose reputations were terrifying: men whose aura marched a step or two in front of them, who were capable of reducing snivelling staff to a state of blubbering incoherence at twenty paces. One of these was John E. Walsh, a large, bald man whose complexion turned florid when he was angry. My father always maintained that Walsh's bark was worse than his bite, and that although capable of verbally annihilating a man face-to-face, he would never hurt anyone behind his back. It was also said that he could tell a story against himself, a saving grace in any human being, never mind a bank inspector. It did little, however, to reduce the awe in which he was generally held.

The usual format of an inspection dictated that the inspector would arrive at the bank without warning after it had shut its doors to the public. He would begin by checking the cash held at the branch, which meant going to the teller and instructing him to stand aside until the job was completed.

In New Ross, Co. Wexford, it happened that the Munster & Leinster Bank and the Provincial Bank stood close together. An inspection was overdue at the Munster & Leinster. On the day appointed, John E. Walsh arrived at the town somewhat ahead of time. Fearing that he would be recognised – surprise being the essential element of the enterprise – he decided to skip lunch, and instead drove his motor car up a quiet lane a mile or so from the town. There, he stopped in the shade of an old chestnut tree and settled down to wait.

At three o'clock as the bank's doors closed, he put the car into gear, double de-clutched (as required by cars in those days) and sped into New Ross. Without the calming effect of a good lunch, he had by now become bilious, transformed into an enraged bull scenting blood and pawing the ground threateningly. He hammered on the closed door of the bank with a roar that carried down the street: '*Inspector!*' The manager and staff fell back in horror. Admitted, Walsh bellowed at thc staff who cowered at the back of the office. He commandeered the teller's cashbox, scattering coins and notes around as he checked the cash, while the terrified teller crouched behind him, trembling. Leaving nothing to chance, he picked up a docket to make some calculations. As he was totting up the figures, he suddenly paused and stared intently at the docket.

'What are you doing with this docket?' he growled at the teller, waving it under the man's nose.

'N…nothing, sir,' the teller said, faintly.

'Nothing? What do you mean "nothing"?' Walsh roared. 'I demand an explanation for this docket immediately!'

'But...' The teller looked confused. 'It's just an ordinary lodgment docket.'

'An ordinary lodgment docket!' The inspector was becoming apoplectic, his face turning bright pink.

'An ordinary lodgment docket!' he repeated. 'And what, young man, is an ordinary lodgment docket from the Provincial Bank doing here in the Munster & Leinster? Can you answer that? What? Speak up, man!'

The teller's voice was almost a whisper. 'But sir,' he breathed softly, 'this *is* the Provincial Bank!'

Walsh's face turned from pink to a startling shade of purple. From the corner of the office, the staff wondered if he were about to have a stroke. They watched, open-mouthed, as he rose to his feet, grabbed his coat and briefcase and swept towards the door, slamming it behind him as he exited. Silence descended. A few seconds passed. Then, from further down the street, they heard the thud of a heavy knocker, followed by an unmistakable roar: '*Walsh! Inspection!*'

~

While the interests, dreams, fears and ambitions of the thousands of young people who took up jobs in the different banks may have been more or less the same, there were distinct variations in the prevailing cultures of the establishments that employed them. When I joined the bank, there were nine clearing banks in the Republic: the Munster & Leinster, the National, the Bank of Ireland, the Provincial, the Ulster, the Royal, the Northern, the Hibernian, and the National City Bank, which had just a single office, in Dame Street in Dublin.

One expression of the cultural differences between the banks lay in their attitude to sport. It is possible that the link between sport and business in Ireland (which some might argue has become unhealthily close today) may even have originated with the banks, where it certainly played an important role in fostering customer relations, as well as providing a useful means of furthering ambitions within the bank. Talent in a particular sport could help a young man's career prospects, as could the social skills for which sport provided a platform, allowing otherwise unlikely social interaction between senior managers and ambitious juniors anxious to make themselves known.

In the 1950s, Gaelic games such as hurling or football were almost exclusively the preserve of the National and the Munster & Leinster Banks. (One obvious exception to this was the great Kilkenny hurler, Eddie Keher, who worked in the Provincial Bank.) If cricket or hockey were your passion, you were most likely to be employed by the Royal Bank or perhaps the Bank of Ireland, or for one of the two banks whose head offices were in Belfast, the Ulster and the Northern. Rugby, once described as a gurrier's game played by gentlemen, was *de rigueur* in all the banks at the time, and to be capped for Ireland was a guarantee of promotion. Soccer ('a gentleman's game played by gurriers') was also widely played, but had yet to make its social mark. Golf was acceptable everywhere – but your status, and sometimes your bank, could be guessed from the club to which you belonged.

In the Munster & Leinster, it began to be seen as vital in retaining the approval of the brahmins of the upper floor in South Mall to participate in the annual golf outing to Mullingar, an event which had come to rival in importance similar outings to Little Island, *the* golf club in Cork. My friends, John Murphy and Dermot Moloughney, who, unlike me, were capable golfers, once persuaded me to attend Mullingar. Our instincts told us that it might be wise to make the pilgrimage at least once.

For a while, the golf went well enough – for my companions, at least. Murphy worked his way diligently down the middle of the course and Moloughney cracked great drives out of sight, while I scuttled back and forth, most of the time looking for my lost ball. At some stage in the day, we arrived at a point close to the first tee, where an admiring group of followers had gathered like a sort of Praetorian Guard around Tom Casey, the influential and highly respected manager at 66 South Mall. Moloughney pulled a driver from his bag. We watched in admiration as, after a few practice swings, he unleashed a powerful drive that saw the ball whirr away elegantly into space. We followed its flight in silence, at first slightly envious, then with creeping dismay, and finally in agonised horror as we realised that it was heading straight for the cranium of Casey, standing on the first tee, oblivious of death heading his way. I uttered a quick ejaculatory prayer. Although punctuated by several involuntary obscenities, it seemed to succeed in deflecting the flight of the missile, causing it instead to skim past Casey's ear, missing it by a millimetre. 'Lads,' he called, in a tone of mild reproach as we nervously drew near, 'you should have shouted "Fore".' We saluted him weakly before mentally collapsing and withdrawing to the bar to restore our nerves.

As the fame of Mullingar spread, bank officials who had been lost for years in remote rural branches came to hear of others who had succeeded in making their mark at the annual golf outing and had moved on to better things. Rusty old irons were hauled out of attics and concentration focused on practising swings. Some would have had to cycle many miles to acquaint themselves again with the feel of a golf course, but there was a general conviction that the effort would pay off.

One man, desperate to escape from exile in the far north-west, was determined to make his bid for deliverance. On arriving at Mullingar, he was teamed up with some ambitious younger bloods, all reasonable golfers intent on showing off their skills. Much to his surprise, he managed to par the first two holes in spite of a set of ancient clubs, several of them rusted by salty Atlantic gales. His luck did not hold, and when someone mentioned that the bank's general manager and his party were breathing down their necks, his nerve cracked, and he began shanking, topping, slicing, hooking, throwing his bag on the greens and forgetting to replace divots. Worse still, his partners, conscious of senior management on their heels, found their own play becoming erratic. Meanwhile, the general manager's game – poor at the best of times – had deteriorated dramatically. With his retinue spending most of their time looking for his ball in the rough, he became liverish and began making unkind remarks about the players ahead of him who were putting him off his form.

Eventually, at the eighteenth green, the main source of the general manager's difficulties was abandoned by his partners. Dejected, he headed for the clubhouse alone. After a wash-up, he considered his position. So far the day had not gone well, but there was still the opportunity to make himself known as an amiable social type, a good mixer who knew how to put his hand in his pocket and stand a round. He headed for the bar to revive his courage and settled down to a few stiff drinks in the company of a Clare man, another first-time pilgrim to Mullingar. With every round he could feel his confidence growing.

A stir was felt in the room. Heads turned. The general manager, slowly recovering from his disastrous game but still feeling peeved, had entered the club lounge surrounded by his acolytes. Our hero, now relaxed, self-assured and exuding goodwill, exchanged meaningful glances with his companion. 'It's now…or never, Seán,' the Clare man slurred. 'Now's your chance!'

Lowering himself from the stool, eyes slightly glazed, Seán made his way unsteadily across the floor and brushed past the outer line of defence, his gaze fixed firmly on the general manager. Standing squarely before him, feet slightly apart, he thrust a hand out in a gesture of manly fellowship. 'Put it there, General Manager!' The general manager stared, but failed to reciprocate. As if detecting a shyness, the man smiled and threw an arm around the shoulders of the bank's highest-ranking executive. Turning to the barman, he roared with an air of authority, 'Joe – a large bottle of stout for the general manager!'

His transfer never came. He had missed the cut on the nineteenth green.

CHAPTER 4

AMONG THE BOLSHEVIKS

As good luck would have it, my own first transfer was to one of the Munster & Leinster's most important branches, in Dame Street in Dublin. To have served in Dame Street carried a certain cachet, and the expression 'Dame Street trained' mysteriously implied a superior grounding in banking.

The Munster & Leinster Bank had an interesting history. It was incorporated in 1884 after the failure of the Munster Bank (which itself had been established following the demise of the Huguenot-established La Touche Bank), and the following year it took over that bank's deposits and some of its branches. The fortunes of the M&L had risen with the foundation of the newly independent Irish state. The bank was a largely nationalist and Catholic institution, although non-Catholic representation, however small, spanned board, management and staff levels. There were certain towns – Killarney, Kinsale, Lismore and Dunlavin, for example – where tradition, long since departed, dictated that the local branch manager would always be a Protestant. This was not because that religion was predominant in the town, but because the area was home to a few important Protestant families who had been customers of the bank for generations.

The link between the Munster & Leinster and the emerging state grew largely out of the involvement of many of the bank's staff in the War of Independence. Typical examples were Keane Harley, manager at Dame Street when I first arrived there, and Brendan Considine, one of the great Clare hurlers of the early part of the century, who had also spent part of his early career in Dame Street. Keane Harley had been an active participant and had been interned for a time in Ballykinler camp in Co. Down. By the time I worked under him in the 1950s, however, all of this already seemed so remote that it was years before I even heard about it.

In January 1922, Michael Collins and William Cosgrave called into Dame Street and formally applied to the deputy manager, J. C. L. Davidson, for a temporary loan of *Twenty Thousand*

Pounds to underpin the finances of the newly-formed government. The request was immediately granted, and Davidson, clearly a shrewd man with an eye to the future, thanked Collins and Cosgrave for bringing the business to Dame Street.

Prior to this, following his tour of the United States in 1919, Eamon De Valera had deposited the funds raised in America in the Munster & Leinster. Despite the British authorities' exhaustive enquiries, the bank maintained client confidentiality. As a result, De Valera became well disposed towards the M&L, and continued even in later years to keep his account in Dame Street, as did several other well-known figures in the struggle for independence. (Padraig Pearse, on the other hand, banked with the Royal Bank of Ireland in Terenure.)

As the new state established itself, public bodies became controlled by nationalists who would have found in the Munster & Leinster a bank broadly sympathetic to their views. Much state-associated business was thus directed towards the bank, which acquired such important accounts as the GAA, the *Irish Press*, certain town and city corporations, county councils, health boards, the cooperative movement and various cultural bodies. In Dame Street alone, personal customers through the years included Sean MacBride, Sean T. O'Kelly and Sean Lemass, and more recently, the latter's son-in-law, Charles Haughey, whose account became the focus of public interest in the 1990s. The various high-profile clients who banked in Dame Street perhaps contributed in some way to the aura of status which attached to working there.

By the time I moved to Dublin in 1954, the Munster & Leinster was well established as the largest bank in the state, with over 150 branches around the country. It was followed closely by the National Bank, with the Bank of Ireland in third place. The Munster & Leinster was unique in that it was the only clearing bank in the country whose head office was in Cork rather than in Dublin or Belfast. It also enjoyed a healthy business in the North, where it tended to be the bank of choice of the nationalist and Catholic community. Even in the Republic, nearly forty years after Independence, it was still decidedly nationalist in outlook, although this was never expressed publicly.

Before leaving Cork, I had been drawn aside by a couple of concerned older colleagues, who, anxious to prepare me for the dangers ahead, had given me some confidential advice. They warned me to be very careful indeed, for not only was Dublin not at all like Cork, but even among the branch staff at Dame Street lurked some who were known to be 'communists'. I didn't know much about communism, but even after five years in the bank my taste for the exotic was still intact, and these warnings only whetted my appetite for whatever lay ahead. My mind on new horizons, I boarded the train at Glanmire Station.

As it turned out, my counsellors in Cork were not entirely wrong, for Dublin was certainly different. It is usual today to depict the 1950s in Ireland as a grey and repressive period. I don't deny that this may have been the reality for many, but it is not how I remember it. Dublin may not have been London or Paris, but to me it was full of activity, novelty and excitement. My early impressions included massed batallions of cyclists poised at a junction at the busiest time of evening, fingers on their Sturmey Archer gears as they waited for a signal from a particularly handsome guard who always seemed to be on duty on College Green. With a wave of his impeccably white-gloved hand, he would send them pedalling on their way around the Bank of Ireland and home to tea.

On frosty nights, long queues hugged the walls for warmth outside the Abbey, the Theatre Royal in Hawkins Street and the Metropole Cinema & Ballroom, which faced Clery's across O'Connell Street. Colourful ice-cream parlours were starting to appear nearby, filled with people tucking into enormous Knickerbocker Glories with long spoons.

The centre of much of the city's high life was the Gresham Hotel, then under the management of the legendary Toddy O'Sullivan. I remember hearing a story he liked to tell about a special dinner organised in the Gresham for a party of Swiss hoteliers. A member of the serving staff had fallen ill shortly before the meal, and a young rookie waiter was brought in to replace him and assigned the task of serving the vegetables. Entering with an enormous silver dish, the young man surveyed the distinguished guests and bellowed across the room, 'Right – hands up the cabbage!'

What delighted me most about Dublin, however, was its citizens. I loved the open warmth, the lack of guile and the humour that I found in the people who lived about me in Crumlin, where my father had become manager of the Munster

& Leinster branch, above which we now lived. On those days when I didn't cycle to work, I caught the bus. The conductor not only collected fares, but called out the stops and delivered his own personalised commentary along the route.

'Scholars for Loreto...on your marks now!'

'Dolphin's Barn – anyone for Fatima?'

'Hold your breath passing Keeffe's, the knackers' yard!'

'Biddy Mulligan! She's in the Coombe...lying in. Ha, ha, ha!'

'Good luck, son,' he would shout, as I jumped off the bus outside the Olympia Theatre.

The bank, too, was different. Where South Mall was measured and sedate, Dame Street was all hustle and bustle. The banking hall had a high, ornate ceiling, with fine old polished counters running in a horseshoe contour around a spacious open area. Within this arc of mahogany, in slightly chaotic conditions, lay the bolshevik encampment of which I had been warned. These were no urban guerrillas. Most of them came from outside Dublin, the sons and daughters of farmers, publicans, gardaí, school-teachers and creamery managers, along with a scattering of bankers' offspring, some of whom, like me, had entered banking through the back door. There appeared to be more women than in Cork, although this may have been a simple reflection of the general increase in the recruitment of female staff that was beginning around this time.

The staff in Dame Street seemed considerably more irreverent and less in awe of authority than the inhabitants of the Mall. Some pushed their iconoclasm dangerously far. Among them was Tim Curtin, a small, wiry man who loved playing with the sound of words and could sometimes be overheard amusing himself at the expense of customers.

'Belly well today, Madam?'

'I beg your pardon?'

'You look very well today, Madam.'

'Oh...thank you.'

'Tickle your arse with a feather, Ma'am?'

'Excuse me – what did you say?'

'Particularly nasty weather we're having...Ma'am.'

On one occasion not long after I joined the branch, another of my new workmates, a young Kerryman, showed himself to be even more audacious. He was dealing with a snobbish woman who wished to open a deposit account, and her superior air had already pushed him to his limit by the time they got as far as completing the necessary forms.

'Can I have your name, please?' he enquired.

'Mrs. Fiona Smythe,' she replied haughtily, spelling it out carefully and pronouncing it to rhyme with 'tithe'.

'And your address, Mrs. Smith?'

'Smythe, young man! The name is *Smythe*, do you hear?'

He eyed her for a second.

'Well, do you know what I'm going to tell you, Ma'am?' he observed conversationally, 'tis an interesting thing now, but in the part of the country I come from (pause) there's about as much difference between Smith and Smythe (pause) as there is between shit and shite!'

Outraged, she stormed off to find the manager's office and complain, and the culprit was dragged in to explain himself and apologise. But he had made his point. I was amazed at such daring.

I soon began to see where the 'communist' label had come from, for there was certainly a core element of militancy in Dame Street whose influence had percolated down in such a way that even the most conservative and mild-mannered among the staff seemed to view authority with suspicion. Not only was it the largest branch of the bank in the country outside of 66 South Mall, but it was also the most active in pursuing the objectives of the union, the IBOA. I have already explained how circulars from Head Office were always couched in careful phrases. Perhaps because of this, they were always carefully inspected by the staff, especially when they related in any way to pay or working conditions, when they would be studied like the entrails of chickens in ancient times for any malevolent omen presaging the banking equivalent of famine, floods or pestilence. Dame Street's resident soothsayer, Joe Doyle, would slowly scrape the sediment from his pipe as he pored over the document.

'What do you think, Joe?' An anxious audience would await his pronouncement.

'I'll tell ye one thing, lads,' Joe would declare grimly. 'This has nothing to do with the tea allowance at all. They're about to put the boot into overtime.'

The manager at Dame Street, Keane Harley, looked exactly like a bank manager should. Comfortably rounded and soberly attired in light grey tweed, he had an avuncular air and an eye said to miss nothing. Nothing in his demeanour would have given even the slightest hint of his past subversive republican activities. His nickname was 'Mandrake' (the magician), and I soon discovered that nicknames were a feature of the office. The deputy manager, Art O'Connor, was 'The Bull', while the assistant manager, Paddy Leahy, who later became an inspector, was known as 'Jakers' ('Jakers, lads – do ye think this is a holiday camp?'). There was also 'The Rebel', 'Shotgun', 'El Mong', 'Blessed Martin', 'Luigi', 'The Buck', 'Mogs', 'The Craven', 'Twinkletoes', 'Tombstone', 'Bongo', 'The Senator', and 'Dollar Bill'.

The origin of some of these names was obvious: Jimmy Manning's dark Italian looks accounted for 'Luigi', and personality quirks lay behind others, but in some cases a name might arise from a single memorable incident. An attempt to get into a dance-hall in Skerries without paying had given Tom Scully his nickname. Having crossed several walls, cut himself on barbed wire and slid down a drainpipe, he finally gained entry through a small window, only to crash heavily on the dance-floor at the manager's feet, clothes torn and blood streaming from his wounds.

'Who the hell are you?' demanded the manager.

Thinking fast, Scully made a desperate attempt at humour. 'The name's Scully,' he growled, in a John Wayne drawl. 'Shotgun Scully, from the Rio Grande.'

The ballroom manager was not amused, but the name stuck.

Deep in the bank's underground vaults, among winding corridors, cloakrooms and toilets, was the porters' lair. This was a small room furnished with a gas ring, a teapot and a kettle continuously on the boil, where the head porter, Martin O'Brien, held court, flanked by his deputy, Edward, and the other porters, most of whom were in some way related to O'Brien. It was a family business and outside of blood circles, only those well connected with him dared to enter.

The vaults had a sort of mystique for me when I first worked in Dame Street. Staff sent down to this underground warren to sort out piles of old ledger sheets might disappear for weeks. Prowling around there myself once, I came across an ancient ledger belonging to the La Touche Bank, which included details of Lord Edward Fitzgerald's bank account. Listed as security against a loan given to another gentleman were some Irish slaves about to be shipped to the West Indies.

Bizarre sounds occasionally wafted up from the depths: the drone of the uileann pipes played by Mick Padian, all-Ireland champion piper, who sometimes used the vaults to practise in. There was also a branch manager from a small town in Clare who would come to Dublin for his holidays and head straight for Dame Street and Martin O'Brien's kitchen, from where his roar could be heard echoing around the vaults, 'O'Brien! Get me a woman!' O'Brien's response was never audible.

CHAPTER 5

BODY AND SOLE

I soon became accustomed to my new surroundings and fell into the routine. For most young bankers, work was humdrum and any chance of promotion consigned to some far-distant future. It depended largely on the number of years service completed, which meant that it could take twenty years to reach the rank of cashier. The manager of a branch in O'Connell Street who discovered a member of his staff reading a newspaper in the vaults and enquired: 'Just what do you think you're doing?' was said to have received the reply, 'Waiting for a teller to die.'

Female staff had to resign upon marrying, a ruling that lasted into the 1970s. A man was expected to advise the bank of his intention to marry and to supply some details regarding his intended spouse. Occasionally the bank would express concern and caution *prudence* in taking such a serious step. The young man also had to convince his employers that he could survive in the married state on a couple of hundred pounds a year.

Despite their meagre salaries, bankers were expected to keep up a respectable appearance. This posed few problems in the anonymity of Dublin, but in smaller towns, it was trickier. Bunny Carr has described an incident where his manager took him to task for slipping up in this respect. The conversation went something like this:

'Carr, you were at the pictures last night?'

'I was, manager.'

'You were downstairs.'

'I was indeed.'

'What were you doing downstairs, Carr?'

'I didn't have the money to go upstairs, manager.'

'Carr, when we don't have the money to go upstairs, we don't go to the cinema – do you understand?'

'Yes, manager!'

One young man with whom I became friendly, Vincent Flynn, used his elderly motor car as his place of residence from May to September, thus making handy savings on rent while enjoying the benefits of a summer retreat in the country. After work he would drive up the Dublin mountains and park beside a stream. He would cook up his tea and go for a long walk, draw the curtains he had fitted in the car, and settle down for a quiet evening with a book (he was an avid reader), followed by a restful sleep. In the morning, he would wash and shave in the stream, drive to Dame Street and park his car in Dublin Castle yard.

Although the bank never expressed its views openly on the matter, religion played a role in our lives, certainly privately and in some sense perhaps even professionally. It is hard to imagine today, but the Munster & Leinster staff organised a weekend retreat every year in the Jesuit house at Milltown or with the Dominicans in Tallaght or Cork. In sparsely furnished rooms with beeswaxed floors, we prayed and plodded about in strict silence from Friday evening to Sunday afternoon. One question which seemed to come up regularly was whether it was sinful to avoid paying income tax. This must have related to an interest in our customers' moral obligations rather than our own, given that we were unavoidably taxed on almost every penny we earned, including the all-important tea allowance of eight shillings and sixpence, to which we were entitled if we had to work overtime.

Membership of the St. Vincent de Paul Society was seen in a positive light, but we ridiculed the shrouded activities of the Knights of Columbanus. In these matters, of course, we were no different to many other workplaces and professional groups at the time. We did not realise it, but we were witnessing the last years of an era in Ireland when religious practice was an integral part of everyday life. A friend of mind once walked unannounced into the office of the Munster & Leinster's general manager, to find him on his knees, rosary in hands, praying 'for the conversion of Russia,' as he explained.

We were permanently short of money. When seriously strapped, we crossed the road to the pub owned by Murt Leonard and his brother Tom beside the Olympia Theatre, where we could cash a post-dated cheque for a few pounds, a procedure seriously frowned upon by the bank. The Leonards ran a place of refuge not only for impoverished bankers, but also for those who toiled in the various government departments in Dublin Castle, and for Corporation officials in nearby City Hall. By the end of the month, Murt, most genial and hospitable of publicans, would hold in his till great wads of post-dated cheques, all awaiting clearance.

Outside of working hours, we did the sort of things most young people did for entertainment at the time. We went to the pictures or to dances in one of Dublin's popular ballrooms: the Metropole, the Crystal in South Anne Street, the Teachers' Club in Parnell Square or the CIE Club in Marlborough Street. The bicycle was our main mode of transport, and cycling as far as Bray to attend a dance was not unusual. If our luck was in, we might end the evening by cycling home with a girl perched on the bar, to be delivered chastely to her front door, where we might be rewarded with a peck on the cheek before turning around to pedal for miles in the opposite direction to get home.

There was also sport, of course, which I have already mentioned. One of my great friends, John Murphy, persuaded me to join Clontarf Rugby Club, obliging me to make a regular round trip from Crumlin to Clontarf for training on a prized twelve-speed racing bike which I sold to him some years later for ten pounds, probably paid off in instalments. After many trials and tribulations, I did on one occasion succeed in making the Clontarf second team.

Murphy was himself a lean machine, all sinew and bone – one of nature's warriors, who took no prisoners on the football field and spoke a language all his own, full of invented words and phrases. His mother had been my father's first love; his father was a bank manager who had died prematurely, after which the family had moved from Cahir to Dublin, where John and his younger brother, Niall, found themselves at home among the non-conformist element in Dame Street.

And there were the pubs. Apart from Murt Leonard's, our regular haunts included Kate MacAuley's in Clanbrassil Street, the Widow Gilligan's in Islandbridge, the Toby Jug near the Gaiety Theatre and O'Neill's in Suffolk Street. Almost everyone I knew smoked and drank – often to considerable excess – and Dublin pubs were the setting for many long evenings of conversation and argument, laughter and song. The company hardly ever included women, since the pub was still largely a male preserve. Most of the girls we worked with, or otherwise knew, seemed in any case either not to drink at all or to confine themselves to a couple of gin and tonics at parties.

The bank's annual Christmas party was the occasion for a certain amount of letting down of hair. Management, full of Christmas goodwill, left itself open to being lectured by junior members of staff well anaesthetised by pints of draught stout in Leonard's, followed by bottles of inexpensive wine paid for by the bank.

There were also many unscheduled parties, particularly in our house in Crumlin, where my parents were in many ways unusually tolerant of the gangs of young people who descended on the house after dances. My brother, Ino, was by this time a priest in the Dominican order, and had gone away to leave me alone and undefended among five ever-laughing, ever-mocking sisters, who ranged in age between thirteen and twenty-two, and who may indeed have at least partly accounted for my friends' readiness to accept any invitation to the Ryan house. Unfortunately, Joyce, Barbara, Helen, Margaret and Susan tended to view my choice of friends with the same jaundiced eye as my mother had done in a previous era.

Dining out was a rare event in those days, even for those who were considerably more affluent than we were. We were still in an era when food was simple: meat, veg and potatoes for dinner, usually eaten in the middle of the day, with chicken as a rare treat on a Sunday. In the evenings, we ate large quantities of bread and tea, sometimes supplemented by eggs, bacon, sausages or tinned sardines, or in summertime, by what passed for salad: lettuce, tomato, scallions, hard-boiled egg and beetroot from a jar. Only the really well-heeled ate dinner in the evening.

The grander still dined out in Dublin's handful of exclusive restaurants, such as the famous Jammet's in Nassau Street, The Red Bank in Westmoreland Street or The Dolphin in East Essex Street, in the area today known as Temple Bar. The restaurants of top hotels like the Gresham, the Royal Hibernian in Dawson Street, or the Russell, which stood on the corner of St. Stephen's Green and Harcourt Street, also fell into the exclusive category.

As for us, when real hunger set in, we would make for the Castle Hotel in Great Denmark Street, famous for its gargantuan mixed grill served on an extra-large plate. Pedalling home from a dance in the early hours, we might stop in at The Manhattan or Molly's Steak House in South Richmond Street for steak and chips, and when Dublin began to discover more exotic fare in the late 1960s, we took to patronising an Indian restaurant called The Golden Orient in Leeson Street. I believe Martin Delaney ('Blessed Martin') and I were probably among the earliest patrons of one of Ireland's first Chinese restaurants, The Imperial in Wicklow Street, still in business today. For romantic evenings, the place to go was a late-night hideaway in Little Mary Street called Alfredo's. There, having rapped on the door and succeeded in gaining admittance, you and the girl of your dreams were led to a candlelit table by Alfredo, with much solicitude and Italian waving of arms, while an out-of-tune piano (occasionally played by my good friend, Vincent O'Dea) did its best to create the desired ambience.

Late one evening as I sat with John Murphy in O'Neill's in Suffolk Street, both of us hungry and seriously short of cash, John suddenly slapped the breast pocket of his jacket with an air of discovery. A satisfied smile spread across his face as he pulled out a rather grubby piece of paper. It was an invitation for two to dine at Michael's, an expensive French restaurant that had opened some months previously in Wicklow Street. His mother had won it in a bridge competition at Clontarf Castle and had passed it over to her son, who had pushed it into his pocket and forgotten about it. Greatly cheered, we pushed our bicycles around the corner and found the restaurant.

Under soft lights, we were ushered to our seats and fussed over by French-accented waiters in dinner jackets and bow-ties, white napkins draped over their arms. A long menu written in French was offered for our consideration. Men of the world, we studied it carefully, unable to understand a word. We considered asking the waiter for his recommendation, but were afraid we might end up with veal brains or some other continental horror. My eye eventually lit on *Sole Bonne Femme*, which seemed like a safe bet: I liked fish, and the 'femme' sounded promising. Murphy opted for the *entrecôte*, and we ordered. The food was delicious: the steak tender, the fish fresh and full of flavour. As our stomachs filled, well washed down by a bottle of wine, our confidence grew. Ah, yes, men of the world. The night was young, and so were we.

Suddenly, out of nowhere, a waiter appeared, looming over us like a large black crow. 'And how is m'sieur's fish?' he enquired in oily tones. It was at this point that a spontaneous phenomenon occurred, one with which I have since grown all too familiar. It is most likely to happen when I have been taken unawares and am required to respond instantly. My mouth opened, and a voice entirely disconnected from my brain addressed the waiter in firm tones.

'I have to say,' it said reprovingly, 'I've had better *Sole Bonne Femme*.'

Across the table, I saw John Murphy's mouth drop open. Choking noises emerged.

The *garçon* went into shock, offered apologies, suggested calling the chef. By now we were both cringing with embarrassment. I desperately tried to shoo him away; insisted that everything was fine; muttered about our having an engagement elsewhere; begged for the bill. It eventually arrived.

'For crying out loud!' said Murphy feelingly, 'Wait till I present them with me mother's bit o' paper!'

I had almost forgotten how we had come to be there. 'You still have it, don't you?' I asked anxiously, as he rummaged in his pocket, where the voucher had lain for several months. Out it came, together with a comb to which it had become attached, stained with Brylcream and shedding dandruff, a filigree of ink spots adorning the upper edge. Murphy attempted to flatten it out before handing it to the waiter with the bill, accompanied by disjointed statements about his mother, Clontarf Castle, bridge, leaking pens.

The waiter stared for a moment or two. He glanced about him with a look of distaste, perhaps looking for a tongs with which to pick it up. Then, holding it delicately away from him between forefinger and thumb, he went off to consult a higher authority. We watched and tried to lip-read as our ticket was held up to the light, studied, turned over and argued about. Finally, the *maître d'hôtel* shrugged in a gesture of Gallic resignation and appeared to scribble a signature. Bicycle clips in hand, we slunk away.

~

In Dame Street, Sean O'Mahony ('The Buck') ran most of the social events. One day, he announced a forthcoming outing to Baltinglass. Tucked away in the Wicklow mountains, Baltinglass had achieved notoriety years earlier when the government, in what was seen by many as a piece of blatant political skulduggery, had attempted to dismiss the local postmistress and install one of its own nominees. The hullabaloo which followed lasted for many months and focused the eyes of the nation on the small town. It became known as the 'Battle of Baltinglass'. O'Mahony had decided that the bank's football team, together with its supporters, would now engage in a sporting and social exercise with the good people of Baltinglass. It would be an amiable coming together of urban and rural, an exercise in building bridges.

Our Gaelic football team was more or less the same motley crew that turned out for every sport. Your chances of being selected were greatly enhanced if you were on friendly terms with the Buck, could be depended upon to pay your round or could sing. On a chilly Sunday morning after early Mass, we assembled and set out for Wicklow under lead-grey skies as if on a voyage of discovery to the upper Amazon. On arrival, an initial parlay with a delegation from the local club made it very clear that although billed as a friendly match, the mountainy men of Wicklow were taking this seriously. The honour of Baltinglass was once again at stake.

Our team looked pale and undernourished as they emerged from the bus in unsavoury-looking togs, a contrast to the hardy, weather-beaten men of the soil who were loping on to the pitch from behind the hawthorn bushes on the far side of the ground, each looking capable of shearing a hundred sheep during half-time. The locals had turned out in force to provide support, their demeanour only marginally less fierce than that of the players. The referee, also a local man, had apparently been selected because he had an account with the bank and was thus expected to be capable of a degree of impartiality.

To a long blast of his whistle and a roar from the crowd, the game commenced. Huddled on the sideline, our supporters were badly outnumbered. They attempted an occasional bleat of encouragement but they were no match for the locals, who roared for bankers' blood as the battle raged up and down the uneven balding pitch. The sound of bone-crunching tackles, yelps and grunts echoed around the hills. Water was brought on frequently to be poured over wounds and down parched throats.

Much to our surprise, our team held its own. Well into the second half and only a point behind, we were awarded a free from the fifty-yard line. Paddy Wall from Cavan, our only inter-county player – whose roars of advice could be heard twenty miles away in Blessington – decided to take the free kick and signalled to Dan Harte to move into the Baltinglass goal-mouth. He floated the ball towards Harte, who leapt high in true Kerry style, only to receive a heavy blow from one of the opposition which flattened him on the ground. Dazed, Harte rose groggily after a few seconds. He looked around, unsure at first of the identity of his aggressor. Then, spotting a Baltinglass player standing suspiciously near him, and with his Kerry blood racing, he lunged and delivered a perfect left hook to the bystander's chin which knocked the man off his feet.

That was it. The crowd invaded. Our linesmen and supporters fled as a pitched battle commenced. While all of this was going on the referee had awarded a penalty kick to the bank, probably for the initial assault on Harte and somehow turning a blind eye to the retaliation. With no one looking, Paddy Wall scored a goal from the penalty spot and drove the ball into an empty net, the goalkeeper being engaged in an altercation elsewhere. The referee, fearful for his safety and perhaps not wishing to undermine a good relationship with bank, blew the full-time whistle and ran for safety.

Gradually the mayhem died down and our team staggered towards the bus while the Wicklow men withdrew with their supporters, claiming a moral victory. There was no 'three cheers for the bank', no invitation to join them in the pub. We learned later that our own feeble support was due in part to the discovery by George Kenny of a local hostelry selling drink at prices well below Dublin's. Abetted by some of our female supporters, George, one of the few Dubliners in the bank and something of a ladies' man in an old-fashioned sort of way, had made a quick decision and decided to skip the sporting side of the event altogether.

The second Battle of Baltinglass was talked about for years. It was not one of the bank's most successful exercises in public relations.

CHAPTER 6

CULTURAL CAPERS

In Dublin, art became my outlet once again, and I was happy to progress to the National College of Art in Kildare Street, where I attended evening classes and availed of the opportunity to learn the techniques of painting from the likes of Maurice McGonigal, Sean Keating and John Kelly. Jimmy Manning ('Luigi') was also a student there, having already studied painting under the noted artist, Bea Orpen, in Drogheda, his previous posting with the bank.

There was something about Jimmy that always reminded me of a heron. He was matchstick thin and angular, with a long neck, prominent Adam's apple and a hooked nose that made him seem watchful, poised and ever ready to swoop. Suspicious of orthodoxy, he approached life as he did art in a highly individualistic way. He was always on the look-out for an opportunity to advance his artistic aspirations. He differed from most other creative souls I knew in one important respect: he was wary of spending money foolishly and often went to considerable pains to avoid it. Sometimes, alas, his efforts would backfire, and tactics intended to achieve economies would frustratingly end up costing him more in the long run.

There was, for example, the matter of the advertisement he once placed in the *Irish Times*. It read: *Wanted: Early Manning paintings*. This cunning scheme failed to provoke the rush on his work or the clamour of interest from the galleries that he had hoped for – and newspaper advertising did not come cheap.

On another occasion, taking exception to the cost of public transport, Jimmy got stuck in Swords while trying to hitch from Dundalk to Dublin. Spotting an out-of-service open-backed bus about to depart for the city without a conductor, he leaped on board unnoticed by the driver and enjoyed a free ride. When he attempted to alight in Gardiner Street, however, he mis-timed the traffic lights and ended up cartwheeling through the air to land heavily on the footpath among a group of women wheeling their prams of fruit home from Moore Street. The street-vendors poured sympathy and maternal concern on poor Jimmy, who was dazed and shocked and had torn the sole of one of his shoes. They insisted on leading him off to a nearby pub to help him recover from his ordeal. By the time they all emerged, hours later, Jimmy had had a very expensive day.

In the office, 'Luigi' tackled the complexities of banking in his own unique style. Twice a year, the bank calculated the interest on customers' overdrafts and loan accounts. It was a complex affair, known as 'averaging', which involved working out the daily balance on accounts, allowing for offsets against credit balances and deposit accounts. Probably done today by computers in a matter of minutes, in those days it demanded weeks of overtime, for which we were always grateful, since the extra money was badly needed. Unfortunately, it also required a grasp of mathematical formulae which neither Jimmy nor I had ever mastered. Jimmy's efforts became works of art, with meandering lines, dribbles and doodles wandering all over the place in the style of a Jackson Pollock canvas. Buried somewhere in the middle were his calculations. I wish I had kept some of them.

Later, Jimmy was transferred to the bank's Barclaycard division, which suited him very well. He was pleased with the mileage allowance, and as he roamed the country recruiting agents for the card, he often found time to pull in by the roadside and sketch the landscapes of the western seaboard which he loved so well. The credit card concept was new to Ireland, and it was the object of much wonder in the small towns of Kerry, Galway and Mayo. Once, Jimmy was surprised to hear of a shopkeeper in Dingle who had apparently been dealing in Barclaycard for years. When he succeeded in tracking him down, the man expressed his astonishment at the bank's attempts to break into the *birthday* card business, which, he assured Jimmy, had long been a 'great take' in Dingle.

I have already mentioned another friend, the great contemporary Irish artist, Tony O'Malley. Like many others who worked in the bank, Tony had spent some years during the Emergency in the Irish army, where he had contracted tuberculosis. He whiled away his long convalescence by painting. Shortly after his return to work in the bank, he began to submit paintings for exhibition and succeeded in having work accepted by the *Oireachtas* and *Living Art* shows in Dublin in 1951, 1952 and 1953.

In 1955, when Tony was working in the bank's New Ross branch in Co. Wexford, Jimmy and I contacted him with a plan to try and organise a joint exhibition of our work. There were very few galleries in Dublin at the time, and it was not easy for aspiring artists to display their efforts in public. We had approached Senator E. A. McGuire, who owned the Brown Thomas store in Grafton Street and was also a distinguished patron of the arts, to ask if we could exhibit in the Little Theatre, the gallery which he had opened in the basement of the famous store and was making available to emerging artists.

In due course, an exhibition was arranged, a date set and O'Malley informed. Some days later, Tony Carpenter, one of the senior porters in Dame Street, approached us bearing a battered cardboard box held together with binder twine, of the type then used on farms for binding sheaves. It had just been delivered from New Ross and looked as if it had barely survived the journey. We tore away the packaging and opened the box. It contained a mesmerising collection of work in oil, pastel, gouache and mixed media. There were even some in the bank's indelible black ink (Mr. Blake would have approved of its everlasting quality). We stared in wonder. Tony had used any material that came readily to hand: canvas, cardboard, paper, backing sheets from the bank's old ledgers. I can still see them in my mind's eye, those paintings of New Ross, Callan and Enniscorthy, of defunct mills, crows, hawks, farmyards in winter. I remember thinking how in tune with one another they were. They had the tang and feel of the Irish countryside, yet I was sure they would look quite foreign and would come as a surprise to many of Tony's colleagues in the bank. Perhaps this was to be expected, for Tony was an unusual man who could appear very ordinary. He had a countryman's quietness that gave no hint of the broad range of his interests, his deeply-held republican convictions and his delightful sense of humour.

Our exhibition in the Little Theatre was opened by John Titterington, general secretary of the IBOA, and we received encouraging reviews from the critics, with particular interest centred on Tony O'Malley. We held another exhibition together the following year in the Dublin Painters' Gallery, a venue that had once been the studio of the artist, Sean O'Sullivan, and is now the café of the Habitat store on St. Stephen's Green, near the top of Grafton Street. Shortly afterwards, Tony left the bank to pursue a full-time career as a painter. Jimmy and I held one further show together, while Tony went on to live for many years as one of an influential group of artists in St. Ives in Cornwall, where he met and married the Canadian artist, Jane Harris. They returned to Ireland in 1990 to settle in a modest house in Physicianstown, a few miles from Tony's birthplace in Callan, Co. Kilkenny, where he continues to produce extraordinary work today.

~

One evening as I sat in Murt Leonard's with my friend, Paddy O'Grady Walshe, the subject of Brendan Behan arose. An occasional patron of Murt's, Behan was creating waves internationally and was seldom off the front pages at home. This had as much to do with his boisterous unpredictability and reputation for hard drinking as with his literary achievements. Most bankers in Dublin at this time were members of the Bankers' Club in St. Stephen's Green, and as we talked about him, we were suddenly inspired to invite Behan to address a club gathering. We had another drink to enable us to get a better grip on the idea, and then settled down to compose a letter. Drafted mainly by O'Grady Walshe and later typed up on official bank stationary, it went as follows:

30th December, 1960

Dear Mr. Behan,

I write at the request of a group of my colleagues who have formed themselves into a committee to provide social and sporting intercourse amongst the staff of this bank in Dublin – not the kind that might spring immediately to one's mind. The idea was born of the belief that for the non-native Dubliner particularly – in the bank at any rate, the shy youngster of 18-20 – this city is a forbidding, unfriendly place. Apart from his colleagues in the bank, our normal Junior's only contacts are with an unsympathetic landlady whose only welcome for him is on pay-day, and so we endeavour to organise inexpensive functions and occasions to help him broaden his outlook and to provide healthy companionship. So far, we have had a film show and a talk on sport; we have got some of them to sing their heads off in a pub; we have got them to give a Christmas party for a group of orphans, and we have got them to travel as spectators and players to two football matches in the country.

I have now been asked to enquire whether you could spare an hour or two at about 7.30 or 8.00 o'clock any evening in the month of January to speak to us on any subject of your choice, or, on our suggestion, 'That modern Irish theatre gets insufficient financial support'.

We have a premises at 93 St Stephen's Green (the Bankers' Club) where we have a room which would hold about one hundred people who would be agog to meet you face to face. None of them is a dramatist, although some are serious theatre-goers; many of them are pseudo-serious pedants until their bluff is called, but they are all trade unionists. We can make them and keep them good trade unionists, but regrettably none of us is competent to contribute to their abysmally slight knowledge of the arts, and we feel that to meet you would be an experience of inestimable benefit to them.

We included my telephone number at the end, and offered to meet him to discuss the matter if he so wished. The letter was signed, somewhat nervously, by me.

News of this plan soon reached John O'Shea, a teller in Dame Street. (His son is the well-known founder of the Third World charity, *Goal*.) I had a great fondness for John, a man of many parts who was to me the very essence of Kerry: intelligent, imaginative and shrewd. His company had enlivened many a dull day for me in the bank. Like Jimmy Manning, John liked to think that he knew how to make a penny stretch, but he reminded me of no one so much as the hero of John Bunyan's *Pilgrim's Progress*, whose soul is in constant battle between vice and virtue as he struggles to attain his paradise. As cashier, he fastidiously cultivated clients whose transactions were in order, but would experience an urgent call of nature when he saw anyone approaching who suggested trouble to his finely-tuned instincts. He had an enquiring mind and a literary bent, and would sometimes engage favoured like-minded customers in discussions on poetry or the philosophy of Canon Hayes of *Muintir na Tire*.

The news of our invitation to Brendan Behan had John worried.

'What's this I hear about ye inviting that Behan fella along to the Club?' he demanded.

'They say he's a great talker, John.'

'A great talker! I'll tell ye something for nothing. That fella has no talent...no talent at all. His work won't last.'

'Do you think, John?'

He could see that his opinion of Behan was not making the desired impression.

'I'll tell ye something for nothing,' he confided, using a well-timed pause to engage our curiosity and create an air of something about to be revealed. 'As it happens, I do a bit of writing myself. In fact, I do a lot of writing.' He nodded, as if agreeing with himself. 'I know what I'm talking about. You (philistines, implied) won't have seen it of course, but I have had an article on James Clarence Mangan published in the *Capuchin Annual*. I know about writing. That Behan fella...he has no talent at all. And what's more, he'll wreck the Club. You'll get into fierce hot water, I'm telling you.'

Days passed and then weeks, with no reply from Behan. Then, one evening, he strolled unannounced into Murt Leonard's and began to bestow the benefit of his wisdom on a mixed bag of topics to the pub's patrons.

'Go on, go and ask him,' my friend, Bob Hurley, urged.

More than a little nervous, I approached the *enfant terrible* of Irish letters and asked politely if he had received our invitation.

'As a matter of fact, I was only looking at it yesterday,' he replied amiably.

Encouraged, I pressed our case. 'Any chance you might be able to oblige?'

He thought for a few seconds. 'Yiz are all trade unionists, aren't yiz?' he mused approvingly. 'Jaze, that was some strike yiz had that time. Yiz were hard men, taking on the banks. Fair enough, then – Wednesday week. Pick me up with Beatrice at the Bailey at seven.'

Success! It had seemed almost too easy – but there was one matter which had not yet been mentioned.

'I'm sorry for asking,' I mumbled, 'but what would you...how much would you be charging for the talk?'

'Listen, son,' came the immediate response, 'aren't we all trade unionists? Don't bother yer arse about the money.'

John O'Shea's gloom deepened when he heard that our

invitation had been accepted. Hadn't Behan caused havoc in the Shelbourne Hotel only the other night? His fears must have transferred to me on some subconscious level, for a few nights later I had a wild nightmare in which an unrestrained, dishevelled Behan invaded the bank, singing rebel songs and waving our letter of invitation about. Hauled before the manager, 'The Bull' O'Connor, I was asked to explain why this document bore my signature, and worse, why it was written on the bank's headed stationery! The horror intensified when Behan leaped upon my inquisitor and began to throttle him, while Martin O'Brien, the head porter, attacked him with a kettle, pouring boiling water all over the manager's mahogany desk in the process.

I awoke in a lather of perspiration, my heart pounding. What if O'Shea were right? I began to have misgivings about the whole affair.

It was decided not to advertise the event: the word was already out. On the appointed evening, Paddy O'Grady Walshe, 'The Buck' O'Mahony and I went along to the Bailey to collect Behan and his wife Beatrice. Brendan looked immaculate in a well-cut dark blue pinstriped suit with matching tie and handkerchief. We asked if he would like a drink before heading up to the Club; to our surprise he ordered a soda water. As we entered the venue, we could sense the anticipation. Most of the bankers we knew in Dublin seemed to be there.

'Good gate this evening,' observed Behan nonchantly, ever the showman.

The meeting room on the first floor was packed well beyond capacity. In the front row, arms folded, sat John O'Shea, grimly awaiting developments. Our guest spoke for almost two hours without a note. He traced his life, outlining his family background. He explained his republican sympathies and politics, and described his arrest and time spent in gaol, going on from there to express his views on international affairs. We listened, enthralled, amused and moved by turns as he spoke about the *Irish Press*; his early plays; his friendships with Joan Littlewood and Louella Parsons; Michael MacLiammoir; and his travels in France with Anthony Cronin. It was a *tour-de-force*, and he had us all in the palm of his hand by the end. My only regret was that, distracted by my anxieties, I had not followed through with my original plan to bring a tape-recorder. No matter – the evening was an unqualified success.

Afterwards, O'Grady Walshe, The Buck and I adjourned with Brendan and Beatrice to the bar, where we commandeered a table. The crowds milled around, all longing to be able to go home boasting of having shaken the hand of Brendan Behan. In no time, John O'Shea had joined us, eager to be involved. He enthusiastically congratulated Behan on his performance.

'Marvellous, Brendan! 'Twas a marvellous talk altogether!'

He went on to engage Behan in a discussion on the problems of writing, having established his credentials as a contributor to the *Capuchin Annual* and a friend of its editor, Fr. Senan. He raised the issue of the demon drink and emphasised, out of his own experience, how it could play havoc with the artistic impulse. He warmly suggested that Brendan should tackle the problem immediately, generously offering to enrol him in the Third Order of St. Francis.

'Wha?' Behan looked bemused.

'The Third Order, Brendan! You'd be involved in all their Masses throughout the world. You'd get fierce grace from it, Brendan, and before long the craving for the drink would pass. I know what I'm talking about – I'm a member myself!'

The evening ended magically in the Paradiso in Westmoreland Street, a smoky candlelit restaurant up a flight of stairs which had become popular as a late-night spot, and where Charles Lynch, one of the country's most gifted pianists, earned just enough to survive by playing popular classical melodies. There we were joined by the actor, T. P. McKenna (a recent escapee from banking) and enjoyed a night of stories and much laughter before putting the Behans into a taxi and making our own way home.

I had barely put my foot in the door of the bank the following morning when an excited John O'Shea came rushing over.

'The man's a genius!' he declared. 'We'll form a cell to study his more recent work...yourself and O'Grady Walshe and George Kenny and Charlie Boland.' (Charlie, a nephew of Freddie Boland, one-time president of the United Nations, and a cousin of the poet Eavan Boland, was a born entertainer who had cheered us on many an occasion with his wit and his music-hall signature tune, *Burlington Bertie*.)

John could hardly contain his new-found enthusiasm for Brendan Behan. 'Yes,' he went on, 'a kind of a literary studies circle! We could meet in Murt's on a Friday evening. He's a genius, I'm telling you. And now that he's packed the drink in, the best is yet to come!'

Some days later, John O'Shea was expounding his views on some favourite topic to a well-heeled customer, a woman dressed in furs whose only wish was to cash a cheque and go shopping. Out of the corner of his eye, he suddenly spotted Behan coming through the main door.

'Oh! – excuse me, Ma'am,' he said importantly, 'I see a great friend of mine who's just come in. I must have a word with him.'

The woman glanced over her shoulder without much interest. She did a classic double-take as she recognised the notorious Brendan Behan.

'Brendan! Brendan!' John called, waving a hand in the air. 'Over here!'

But he had failed to notice something. This was a different Brendan Behan.

'O'Shea, ya black Kerry hoor!' he roared, lurching in the direction of the open-mouthed cashier. His jacket was torn and a stained tie hung loosely half-way down his chest, much of which was visible thanks to a missing button on his filthy shirt. This was the thundering, rampaging, very drunk Brendan Behan of whom we had been warned at the outset.

'O'Shea!' he repeated. His voice carried all over the building. Heads went up, people emerged from behind closed doors, customers stared. 'What about the Third Order, O'Shea?' he demanded. 'Come back here, ya hoor's ghost!'

The last I saw of the chairman of the Brendan Behan Study Group was his retreating back as he fled to the safety of the vaults. As he shot past, he muttered in my direction, 'What did I tell you? No talent...no talent at all!'

~

Before I knew it, nearly four years had passed in Dame Street. I was not the only exile from Cork there. Among the attendance at the Brendan Behan lecture that night was a tall, attractive young woman who had recently been transferred from South Mall. Like so many of my friends, she was the product of a banking background, and her father worked in the Munster & Leinster in Macroom, where he later became manager.

I soon discovered that Mary Cahill had a great sense of fun and a capacity for enjoying life. She also had an independent mind with definite views on most things, and unlike me, had her feet planted firmly on the ground. Opposites attract, the saying goes, and in our case, it was probably true. Love blossomed as we started 'doing a line', which seemed to consist mainly of going to the pictures or the theatre, in which Mary had a special interest, not least because her mother wrote short stories and plays for radio and the theatre, and had even had a play staged at the Abbey. On summer evenings or at weekends we sometimes took the bus out of the city to enjoy a trek in the Wicklow mountains, and there were many visits to the Ryan house in Crumlin, where my family welcomed her with open arms.

Anyone who watches nature programmes on television will have seen birds and other creatures woo a mate with elaborate offerings. *Homo sapiens* does it with flowers, jewellery, chocolates and the like. As for me, I once presented myself to Mary's landlady in Harold's Cross with a brown paper bag containing two enormous lamb chops. Mary was confined to bed at the time, recovering from a bout of 'flu, and I thought she could use the vitamins. Handing the bag to the startled landlady, I indicated that one of the chops was for the invalid. 'The other one,' I added pleasantly, 'is for me.' The look on the woman's face made it clear that she was *not* in the habit of cooking meals for her tenants, and *certainly* not for their friends.

A woman of fainter heart might have given up on me at that point. Mary didn't. We married in June 1961, in Douglas, Cork, and spent our honeymoon in London at the house of my sister, Helen, who was conveniently away on holidays. We returned to begin married life in the gate-lodge of an old estate house in what was then open countryside near Shankill, a few miles from Bray, which we rented for ninety pounds a year. Our three boys, John, Eamon and Robert, arrived in rapid succession, followed by our only daughter, Marion. They have all had a lot to forgive, but they will be relieved to know that they have been spared a further mention in these pages.

CHAPTER 7

T'RUPPENCE EACH DE STARLIGHTS

My next transfer, to Mary Street, came shortly after I got married. The Mary Street office of the Munster & Leinster was not officially a branch at all, but a sub-office of Dame Street – a sort of chapel-of-ease north of the river to that great banking cathedral. If Dame Street represented a change for me after Cork, it was nothing to the effect of Mary Street after Dame Street. I learned more about real life there in a couple of years than in all my previous time in the bank.

In Dame Street, the customers we dealt with day-to-day across the counter were mostly businessmen and their secretaries; civil servants from Dublin Castle; employees of Dublin Corporation; fashion-conscious shoppers bound for Grafton Street; and the occasional politician or bishop. On one memorable occasion we were visited by the recently-appointed cardinal archbishop of Armagh, Dr. Conway, who surprised us by arriving unannounced. Alerted by a diligent member of staff, the manager, Art O'Connor, rushed out to greet him. Unfortunately, in his eagerness to kiss the archbishop's ring, he slipped and instead succeeded in cracking his jaw on the counter, ending up prostrate on the ground before the startled archbishop, who had to help him to his feet before submitting to being led away to the dazed manager's office.

This was Dame Street. The faces became familiar, but with rare exceptions we did not know the people.

Mary Street was a different place entirely. The premises itself could at best be described as unpretentious. It held no more than about a dozen customers and its furnishings were limited to an aged safe, a single telephone and a couple of storage heaters. To get to the toilet or the small room upstairs you had to pass through the manager's office, which itself was little more than a cage of frosted glass behind the counter.

Apart from the manager and the porter, the staff in Mary Street numbered four or five at the most. Among them was Bob Hurley, another banker's son formed by a nomadic childhood. His gift with words and his quick-fire sense of humour made him a wonderful companion, and we developed a close friendship that lasted until his untimely death in 1987.

Since there was room behind the public counter for only two or three staff at a time, the queues that developed often moved quite slowly. The customers never seemed to mind. They kept us amused with the latest yarns and jokes, and Bob and I did our best to reciprocate. I remember one morning crouching together out of sight behind the counter as the first customers filed in, rising, Tommy Dando fashion, to regale them with a rousing chorus of *Keep Your Sunny Side Up*. (Dando was the organist at the Theatre Royal in the days when both organ and organist would magically appear on a mechanically operated platform that emerged from a trapdoor in the orchestra pit, in the interval between the stage entertainment and the film.) The customers responded to this unexpected musical welcome to the bank by enthusiastically joining in.

Most of our customers had infinitely more trouble-ridden lives (we hadn't yet discovered the concept of 'stress') than those who frequented Dame Street, but they had a knack for turning what others might have regarded as time wasted in queuing into an opportunity for catching up on gossip, passing on tips for a dog running in Shelbourne Park or exchanging remedies for piles and chilblains. The clientèle was largely made up of small retailers, publicans and the weather-beaten women who sold fish, 'ri-ep' oranges, apples and 'pay-ers' on Moore Street; or the wily characters who kept a sharp eye out for prowling gardaí while selling tobacco and knicknacks out of suitcases, and who ran in frequently to change a five-pound note or proposition the manager for a small loan. Over time, we got to know them all, becoming familiar not just with the state of their finances but often with the details of their lives, which they had few inhibitions about sharing.

The manager of the branch, Brendan Conroy (we called him J. B.), was entirely in keeping with the spirit of the street. One of the few Dubliners working in the Munster & Leinster, he was bald with a bristling moustache and the appearance of a man not to be trifled with. In reality, J. B. was easy-going, generous and warm-hearted, with a fine singing voice and a wicked sense of humour. He enjoyed company and was fond of late-night socialising, which may have explained the ruddy complexion that sometimes contributed to the initial impression of irascibility.

Before taking up his post in Mary Street, J. B. had been in charge of personnel in Dame Street, where his views on staff relations included some original ideas. He was once heard to remark that most of the problems in the bank could be put down to an over-sexed staff, although I never heard him expand on this theory.

He owned an elderly Volkswagen Beetle which frequently ran out of petrol at inappropriate times and places. Every morning he would begin his working day by driving the car up on the footpath outside the bank in Dame Street, where he would collect a tin box containing the cash needed for the day in Mary Street. His assistant's first task was often to fill the tank from a spare can of petrol which J. B. kept in the boot. Since the car was seldom washed, it was difficult to see through the front window (it did not help that one wiper worked only intermittently). Peering through the dirt and driving at a steady ten miles an hour, J. B. would depart for Mary Street, swearing loudly at the bad driving habits of Dublin motorists. On arrival, he would once again drive up on the footpath, disembark and ease his way past the queue that was building up outside, searching in his pockets for the keys to open the bank. With the crowd milling around, J. B. would invariably get drawn into conversation with someone with a good joke to tell or an urgent financial problem to discuss, forgetting the car with the door still open and the cashbox on the passenger's seat.

The inhabitants of the area around Mary Street included members of the Jewish community. They added colour and brought their own unique sense of humour as a worthy challenge to the quick wit of the native 'Dubs' by whom we were otherwise surrounded. On one occasion we were confronted by something even more exotic in the form of a diminutive man with oriental features. He probably came from one of the Chinese restaurants that were beginning to appear around the city at the time, but since he did not speak a word of English, Bob and I struggled in vain to grasp the precise nature of his enquiry. The arrival of J. B. on the scene, flushed from the effects of a late night in Delgany Golf Club, did little to improve matters. Conroy's approach seemed to be to adopt a peculiar version of English whose intonations attempted to mirror those of the foreigner. Strange sounds issued from both parties but little progress was made. Meanwhile, the interested customers did their best to be helpful.

'He's prob'ly lookin' for a lo-an, Misther Conroy,' observed one.

'No, he's not,' retorted another, cannily noting a brown paper bag sticking out of the gentleman's pocket. 'He wants ta put money on deposit.'

Following the customer's downward glance with his eyes, Conroy brightened visibly at the idea of a new account, and he immediately reached for a signature card and pen which he pushed towards the man with a gesture indicating what was required. The man obliged, and returned the card. J. B. studied it for a few minutes in silence, his moustache moving doubtfully. Finally he looked up again and regarded the signatory with a frown.

'What's all this about?' he enquired testily.

'It's his sig-enature, Misther Conroy!' one of the customers interjected in the background.

'Listen, son,' said J. B., not unkindly. 'This is how we sign our names here,' (writing in the air with an emphasis on the left-right horizontal movement). 'Supposing another…another…well, someone that looked like you…came in to take money out of this account, how would we know if it was you or not – what? And how are we ever going to recognise this signature?'

The situation was finally resolved with the help of elaborate sign language and role-play, when the combined efforts of Bob and I (assisted by the customers) eventually succeeded in impressing upon the little man that he must always present himself to Conroy in person when he wished to withdraw or lodge money. J. B. meanwhile concentrated on studying the new customer's features intently and trying to commit them to memory. For all his gruffness, he always responded to people with a genuine human heart rather than out of any schooled professional consciousness.

J. B.'s mother paid periodic visits to carry him off to some destination never revealed to us. The timing was wrong for it to involve lunch, and clearly they did not simply go somewhere to enjoy a quiet cup of tea together, since he was often seen to make tea on his return to the office. Then, one morning, she arrived in the bank while J. B. was in closed session with a customer, and since it was raining outside, she had no option but to sit down and wait. As time went by, I noticed her repeatedly looking anxiously at the wall-clock. Finally, she approached me.

'Do you think Brendan will be much longer?'

'I'm sure he'll only be a few minutes, Mrs. Conroy,' I reassured her.

'I hope you're right,' she said, glancing at the clock again. 'It's just that...confessions in Dominick Street will be over if he doesn't hurry.'

A moment later, Conroy emerged, putting on his hat and overcoat. 'Right, Ma – I'm ready,' he announced, and off they headed in the direction of the Dominican Church.

Brendan Conroy was the softest of soft touches. He lent the bank's money – and often his own – liberally. As word spread about his approachability, sharp-looking characters with turned-up collars would appear in the bank and sidle up to the counter. Glancing suspiciously over their shoulders, they would speak out of the corner of their mouths: 'Are you Misther Conroy? Anto said I should have a word. I'm his furst cousin, Lar.'

J. B. was also an easy target for the neighbourhood's hard-luck cases. One of them, a down-and-out by the name of Henry Murphy, called every day. Henry occasionally spent the night in a local hostel, but in spite of J. B.'s efforts, mostly he slept rough, even on the coldest winter nights. J. B. gave him money every day – and expected us to provide a shilling or two as well. The five-day working week was introduced around this time, and on the day before the first Saturday when the bank would be closed, Henry turned up with a slightly worried look on his face.

'Misther Conroy,' he enquired, 'I hope ya don't mind me askin', but will I be gettin' me Sathurday money along with the Friday from now on, seein' as yis won't be here on the Sathurday?'

Occasionally Henry would appear looking very much the worse for wear, having spent a bad night on a park bench or in a doorway. One winter's morning when it had been raining very heavily, he came in soaked to the skin and collapsed into a chair beside one of the storage heaters, where he immediately fell asleep. In minutes, he was enveloped in a cloud of steam as the heat from the storage heater warmed his saturated clothes. Willie Wade, the porter, looking a little concerned, asked J. B. if he should wake him up and get him a cup of tea. J. B. shook his head. 'No, Willie, leave him alone. He needs a good kip. He can go and get a ball of malt when he wakes up.'

As Henry slept and the steam rose around him, a bedraggled pigeon suddenly walked through the open door, trickles of water running down its feathers. It headed straight under Henry's chair, where it calmly settled down and proceeded to preen itself. It was an extraordinary moment: two battered creatures companionably sharing a temporary refuge in a bank. No one stirred. No one spoke. We all felt strangely moved. After a few minutes, the pigeon stood up, shook itself as if to say, 'That's better,' headed jauntily towards the door and vanished. With awe in his voice, Willie broke the silence: 'Wasn't that amazin', Misther Conroy!' And it was.

Willie lived in nearby Dominick Street and suffered from asthma, which did nothing to diminish his appetite for work. It was dangerous within Willie's hearing to drop a casual remark such as, 'We should probably get this stuff over to Dame Street one of these days,' for before you knew it, Willie would be on his way, pedalling determinedly along Capel Street with his load strapped to the carrier of his bike. Days would often go by before the items would be missed.

One day, J. B. decided that customers with substantial cash lodgments to make should be encouraged to transact their business in the converted bedroom on the first floor, where a temporary teller could deal with them, freeing space and staff on the ground floor. Willie's role would be to acquaint them with this new facility and lead them upstairs.

One afternoon a few weeks later, as a queue was forming in front of me, I noticed a striking young woman clutching a large handbag three or four back in the straggling line. Even at a glance it was obvious from the cut of her clothes and her general demeanour that she was not from the area. My guess was that she had probably strayed in from the leafier regions of Foxrock. Willie, attired in a faded sports-jacket (he never wore a uniform), must have spotted my quizzical look. He sprang to his feet and following my gaze, sized up the young woman with the handbag before turning towards me again. Our eyes met, and Willie baffled me by first giving me a conspiratorial nod and then crossing the floor to approach her.

'Excuse me, miss,' he addressed her.

'Yes?'

He lowered his voice discreetly, and I had to strain my ears.

'Would you care to go upstairs?'

The young woman looked startled. 'I beg your pardon?'

'Upstairs,' he repeated. 'We've a special room up there now.' He winked.

She looked around nervously and began to flush, but said nothing. Willie, however, was nothing if not dedicated. He caught her arm gently.

'The back bedroom,' he said. 'There's a man up there who can handle you. I'll show you the...'

But before he could get any further, the girl had turned on her high heels, which could soon be heard clickety-clacketing furiously on the footpath as she fled in the direction of Henry Street and the safety of Arnott's. We were still laughing at closing time.

Bank robbery was virtually unknown in Ireland up until the early 1970s, when the escalating trouble in Northern Ireland soon made it almost an everyday event. It seems extraordinary in the security-obsessed world we live in today, but in the branch in Mary Street, where space was in short supply, we had no qualms about piling up the daily cash brought over from Dame Street in a convenient spot next to the window that looked out on the street. A few faces occasionally pressed against the glass, but nothing ever happened until one December morning in 1963, when a man in a sheepskin jacket suddenly grabbed a bundle of notes from the counter and fled into the street.

Almost before I knew what I was doing, I had leaped over the counter and was giving chase, quickly followed by Bob Hurley. Dodging through the crowd, the thief sprinted up Mary Street towards Liffey Street, his yellow coat a complete give-away even among the crowds. As I ran, a phrase from my childhood comics came back to me and I found myself yelling, 'Stop thief!', probably to the amusement of the bystanders. Behind me I could hear Hurley's pounding feet, heavy breathing and some rather more colourful expressions than those found in children's comic books. The chase continued up Middle Abbey Street, where the thief's luck gave out. A young garda suddenly appeared out of nowhere, shot past me and caught up with him outside the offices of the *Irish Independent*. I arrived on the scene just ahead of a fuming Hurley, who had to be restrained from attacking the man on the spot. To the acclaim of the crowd which had gathered, we all headed back to the bank, the garda frogmarching the robber, to find J. B. and Henry standing on the doorstep. 'What the hell do you fellas think you're up to?' J. B. growled, as if we'd been out enjoying an unauthorised mid-morning stroll.

The man was searched and relieved of £500. In no time, press photographers and journalists began to appear. Five hundred pounds snatched from a bank? – this was a major news story. It made the front pages, and that evening the TV cameras turned up at our house in Dundrum, where I was interviewed for the news.

Some thirty-five years later, I found myself in conversation one evening with the deputy commissioner of the Garda Siochana, Tom O'Reilly, whom I had come to know in the meantime. Our talk turned to armed robbery, and I mentioned the Mary Street incident. He seemed interested. As I proceeded to tell the story, he looked at me curiously. 'Do you remember the name of the guard who caught the thief?' he interrupted. I didn't. I wasn't sure I'd even heard it at the time, although it had probably appeared in the newspaper reports. 'It was me,' he said, laughing. 'So you were the skinny one flying up the street! I remember it well.'

~

At Christmas-time the Mary Street area really came to life. Along Henry Street, trade in 'starlights', tinsel, 'wrappin' paper', cheap crackers, 'balloo-ins' and Christmas novelties boomed. The raucous voices of the traders carried on the cold December air as they roared to advertise their wares and outdo each other with bargain offers.

In the bank, special customers dropping in on J. B. would be invited into his office, and the sound of clinking glasses and hearty laughter would soon invade the public area. Christmas was a good time for managers. Grateful customers would take the opportunity to express their appreciation, and bottles of whiskey, brandy, gin and wine would begin arriving early in December. Occasionally some other gift might appear, perhaps a present from someone whose overdraft had been increased or renewed during the year. In general, these expressions of goodwill did not extend to the staff, so I was very pleasantly surprised one year, shortly before closing time on Christmas Eve, when a butcher's mate from one of the better shops on Moore Street walked into the bank, looked around, seemed to single me out and walked up to the counter to deposit a fine turkey on the counter before me.

'Happy Chris'mis!' he said, cheerfully. 'Misther Simmonson wants ya ta have dis, for all de good turns ya done us durin'de year.'

I thanked him profusely and said I would ring Mr. Simmonson, with whom I had regular dealings, to thank him personally.

The butcher's mate laughed. 'Ye'd be wastin' yer toi-ime,' he said. 'He's finished up for de day and gone for a bi' of a gargle, ya know yerself!' He winked. 'But sure ya can tank him after de Chris'mis,' he added. 'Ye'll be able ta tell him how much yis enjoyed de burd.'

'De burd' turned out to be one of the best ever eaten in the Ryan household. And so, on the first day of opening after Christmas, when I raised my head from counting notes and saw Mr. Simmonson entering the bank, I prepared to be effusive in my thanks. Simmonson, however, gave me little more than a passing glance before heading straight in the direction of J. B. Conroy.

'Happy New Year to you!' he greeted him.

'And a prosperous one to yourself, Mr. Simmonson,' J. B. responded.

'Well?' said Simmonson, 'And how did the bird go down?'

Conroy regarded him with a slightly puzzled air: 'The bird? What bird?'

'The turkey!' said Simmonson. 'The one I sent up to you on Christmas Eve.'

My mouth fell open…and J. B.'s quick eye spotted it, and my dismayed expression. There was a moment's hesitation. His moustache twitched. 'Oh, *the bird*, you mean!' His eye caught mine. '*That* bird!' 'Well!' he declared warmly, 'that, Mr. Simmonson, was actually one of the finest turkeys I have ever eaten! A terrific bird altogether. Now, come in and have a tincture with me in honour of the New Year.'

As he led his customer into his office he cast a final meaningful glance across his shoulder at me, and I knew I would be hearing about Simmonson's turkey for a long, long time to come.

CHAPTER 8

A CHANGE OF DIRECTION

The 1960s ushered in a period of huge change in banking in Ireland. It had begun a little earlier, in 1958, with the purchase by the Bank of Ireland of the Hibernian Bank, one of the smaller of the nine Irish clearing banks and essentially a Catholic institution. The Bank of Ireland, by contrast, had long been a pillar of the old Anglo-Irish establishment and was very much a Protestant bank. Its acquisition of the Hibernian marked the beginning of the leavening of that image, at a time when it had fallen into third place nationally behind the Munster & Leinster Bank and the National Bank.

An important contributor to the process of change, both in banking in general and specifically in the Bank of Ireland, where he became governor in 1965, was Don Carroll of the P. J. Carroll Tobacco Company. Before his arrival on the scene, Irish banking had no obvious spokesman, and despite the banks' immense power, they had little public voice. Carroll filled that vacuum and caught the popular imagination. In media terms, he was quotable, with definite ideas on the future of banking and little fear of controversy. As the 1960s unfolded, he entered into discussions with John Leydon, a director of the National Bank who was also Sean Lemass's protégé in masterminding the country's industrial development. Together, Carroll and Leydon quietly began to plan the purchase of the National Bank by the Bank of Ireland.

Meanwhile, the directors and executives of the Munster & Leinster Bank in its heartland in Cork seemed oblivious to events in Dublin. Happy in the knowledge that the M&L had become one of the country's two leading banks, they had taken their eye off the ball. Their sole director in Dublin, David Coyle, was a pious and abstemious man who did not frequent the smoke-filled clubs and locker rooms where rumours of takeovers and intrigue might circulate. Thus, when the Bank of Ireland announced in 1966 that it had purchased the National Bank, the news came like a bolt from the blue. Many of the National Bank's staff seemed to feel that if consolidation were indeed inevitable, the National's culture would have integrated more naturally with the

Munster & Leinster's than with that of the Bank of Ireland, a view that was reciprocated by their counterparts in the M&L.

Of the remaining clearing banks, the Munster & Leinster, the Provincial and the Royal Bank of Ireland now faced a competitor with assets worth £300m and a wider branch network than any of them. Very different in their respective cultures and business mix, but forced by the pace of events around them, they began to parlay behind closed doors. In September 1966, they formed a holding company, *Allied Irish Banks*, with assets totalling £250m, of which the Munster & Leinster's stood at £148m; the Provincial's at £72m; and the Royal's at £35m. It was agreed that the three banks would continue trading separately under their existing names. The holding company's registered office was the Munster & Leinster branch in Dame Street. Its first chairman was Edmond O'Driscoll (popularly known as 'Mon'), a Catholic stockbroker from Belfast. O'Driscoll had established an industrial finance company that had subsequently been bought out by the M&L, and a seat for him on the board of the bank had been part of the deal.

Allied Irish Banks began operating from a small office over a branch of the Munster & Leinster at 52 Upper Baggot Street, with a staff of five under its first chief executive, Brendan Harty. Together, Harty, Joe McGlinn, Michael Kennedy, Dick Barrow, Derek Motyer and Joan Geraghty became known as the 'Pembroke Six'.

By 1969 it was clear that the way forward lay in full integration. Under the guidance of Mon O'Driscoll and Niall Ebrill (who by then had taken over as chief executive), the three banks merged operations and began trading under the name of the holding company, Allied Irish Banks. Its first head office was in Lansdowne House in Dublin, at the junction of Lansdowne Road and Northumberland Road. The final amalgamation took place in 1972, when the names of the three individual banks disappeared forever off the country's banking map.

All of these happenings were viewed by the staffs of the banks with a predictable mixture of apprehension, opportunism and indifference. There was the usual handful who spotted a chance for advancement and got ready to storm any passing bandwagon. Others, fearing they had strayed into dangerous waters, floundered about making brave noises and hoping they might be hauled aboard a lifeboat. The remainder simply wanted to retain their jobs and status, and were not greatly concerned about the precise name or shape of the establishment employing them. One question was of interest to everyone, however: who was *really* calling the shots? The Munster & Leinster was the chief suspect, but it was hard to be sure. As at the reading of a will, anxieties and suspicions were rampant. Inheritances were scrutinised and opinions delivered. Depending on the particular issue and the institution one came from, things were judged 'fair', 'not fair' or 'a bloody disgrace'.

For the bank, bedding down the three establishments into something resembling a coherent entity was not without its challenges. With their very different histories and cultures, the banks had shared the same streets in towns and villages for years in a spirit of competition. The country was littered with former Provincial Bank managers who were still smarting because Denis McCarthy, Ireland's first agricultural relations officer in banking, had skilfully captured the business of almost every cooperative and mart in the country for the Munster & Leinster.

In Northern Ireland, the Munster & Leinster's business was Catholic and Nationalist; the Provincial's Protestant and Unionist. The new bank now found itself with branches cheek-by-jowl in 'Derry' and 'Londonderry', with staffs who barely recognised one another. Indeed, certain Provincial officials were rumoured to regard the staff of the M&L as 'muck-savages', who probably ate their young. The Royal Bank of Ireland, meanwhile, had monuments in many of its offices to staff who had lost their lives on behalf of king and country in two World Wars ('*Royal boys were loyal boys*,' was a well-known refrain); while so respected were the M&L's credentials as a supplier of combatants in the War of Independence that one man had succeeded in obtaining a state disability pension for a wound received 'during 1916' – never mind that it had been inflicted in the Battle of the Somme.

As if this were not enough, there was the public to be reassured, as well as the shareholders. A new logo appeared, reflecting the Holy Trinity-like composition of the new entity, but the bank undoubtedly faced a problem that was not going to be solved by a small emblem already in danger of being confused with that of the Mercedes motor company. A new buzzword began to circulate in the bank: *communication.* It had a thoroughly modern ring. It was decided that here lay the key to the threatened identity crisis. Branches were suddenly flooded with circulars, account-holders were mailed, and an advertising campaign got under way with the newly coined slogan: *Three Great Banks in One*. (The Munster & Leinster had already dabbled in press advertising in a limited way, but traditionally banks would have frowned on advertising as liable to encourage unsuitable applicants to want to open accounts!)

On the staff side, management decided that a formal gesture was needed to bond the disparate group, and someone eventually came up with an idea. A party would be held – nay, a series of monster parties, in different parts of the country, to which even the lowliest members of staff would be invited. These parties would be attended by a travelling show of Allied Irish Banks' most senior executives, including the chief executive, who would address the ranks from the podium. The mood would be one of welcome, reassurance and cherishing, of equality and transparency, optimism and new dawns.

The largest halls were booked and diaries checked. Scriptwriters were put to work on carefully worded speeches that were designed to rally the masses while keeping a wary eye on the union, the IBOA, which could be relied upon to scrutinise every word and commit to long-term memory anything resembling an assurance that might have to be fulfilled at a later date.

In Dublin, the venue chosen was the RDS. Rumours of a free bar had greatly enhanced the level of interest, and bankers turned out in force, many of them meeting up well beforehand in nearby pubs. By the time the event got under way, the assembly was already bonding marvellously, the chief concern being that the speeches should not take too long and unduly interrupt the bonding process.

When the speeches and the official business of the evening were finished, the word regarding free refreshments proved true beyond anyone's wildest dreams. There was an apparently never-ending flow of brandy, whiskey, vodka, rum, gin – even exotic cocktails, for anyone so inclined. This was the bank at its most munificent. Impressed by the hospitality, we were anxious to show our appreciation. Habitual bottle-of-stout men abandoned tradition, and cries of 'A large brandy, please!' and 'Make that a double!' rang around the bar. In no time at all, latent hostilities towards integration had abated; inhibitions had vaporised and a feeling of general goodwill prevailed. Senior executives mingled in a spirit of *noblesse oblige* with the *hoi polloi*, leaving at least one young recruit to wake up next morning wondering why his new-found friend of the night before – to whom he had confided some of his more outrageous opinions on the merger – had later been spotted hurriedly leaving the RDS grounds in a chauffeur-driven car.

Whether by accident or by cunning design, the evening was a glorious success: it is still talked about by those who were there, although curiously enough, it was hard to find anyone who could remember much of the chief executive's address even a few weeks later. It occurs to me in retrospect that in its anxiety over our differences, management had probably overlooked the fact that the staffs of the three banks had more to unite than to divide them. In particular, we were all members of the IBOA, whose main concern was to better our working conditions, and *that* was what mattered more in the end than any symbolic or cultural allegiances.

~

In step with events going on about me, my own life took an unexpected about-turn around this time. In the winter of 1968, I came down with what at first seemed like nothing more than a 'flu. Although I had almost died at birth (my torso still bears the scar of a life-saving operation carried out by a doctor with a carving knife on our kitchen table in Tramore), I had almost never been ill, and in my mid-thirties, and finally filling out from the scarecrow skinniness that had plagued me since childhood, I took my health for granted. It was therefore a bit of a shock to discover that a potentially serious virus was apparently eyeing my heart muscles with interest. The result was a stay in Mercer's Hospital, my main memory of which is receiving a pint of freshly-pulled draught Guinness, carefully carried from the pub around the corner beneath the overcoat of a concerned friend, John Casey.

This potent remedy, combined with medical care and various antibiotics, seemed to do the trick. I recovered and soon returned to work, where the bank suddenly decided to move me back to Dame Street. Perhaps they feared that chasing bank-robbers and lifting heavy bags of coins could become habits injurious to my health, for I was no sooner back in Dame Street than I was offered a new position there. It was one that removed me forever from behind the counter, and thrust me into a new area in banking. As so often, I had somehow fallen squarely on my feet, this time landing in the brave new world of public relations.

Public relations in the 1960s, in Ireland at least, was still in the process of inventing itself. The manager in Dame Street at this time was Frank Dorgan, a Cork man with an independent turn of mind who had all the style of one of that city's merchant princes. His previous posting had been in Galway, where he had persuaded the board of the bank to restore Lynch's Castle, the historic building that housed a Munster & Leinster branch in the centre of the city. One day in 1969, Frank called me into his office, briefly outlined the role of public relations as he understood it, explained why he believed the time had come for the Munster & Leinster to explore its possibilities, and entrusted me with responsibility for doing so (without, I might add, any authorisation whatsoever from Head Office). A few days later I was released on to the streets of Dublin and left to my own devices.

I attacked the mission with a mixture of trepidation and enthusiasm. Day One saw me making for Burgh Quay and the Silver Swan, a pub known to be frequented by journalists. By way of training, I had received what turned out to be a most valuable piece of advice from Denis McCarthy, the bank's head of agricultural relations: 'Use all of your ears and half of your mouth, and you won't go wrong'. I set out to put this formula to the test. Arriving in the Silver Swan around noon, I pulled up a stool. After a while, a bird-like man sitting nearby glanced my way. In a well-honed ritual of Irish pub etiquette, he caught my eye and aimed a barely perceptible, sideways nod of the head in greeting towards me. A moment's silence followed.

'So...' He folded his arms and prepared to get down to business. 'What brings you to this den of iniquity?'

'I've landed a new job...to do with press relations,' I ventured.

'Oh?' He looked interested.

'With the Munster & Leinster Bank.'

'Oh?' His eyebrows registered surprise. He looked me over for a few seconds, then pushed his stool back in a gesture of invitation to join the bedraggled-looking group with whom he had been discoursing. 'Well, then – welcome to the Mucky Duck. (It took me a few seconds to register the Silver Swan's *alter ego*.)

'I'm Noel Conway,' he added amiably. 'Come on, I'll introduce you to the club.'

I couldn't have hoped for a better start. Noel Conway had a weekly column in the *Irish Press* and he knew the Dublin wing of the fourth estate intimately. I didn't know it, but my new life had begun.

Before I had fully settled into the job, however, another couple of events took place which resulted in a further change of direction. The first, already described, was the absorption of the Munster & Leinster into AIB. The birth of this new force – which coincided with the dawn of a new era of confidence, prosperity and openness to outside influences in the country generally – saw the old order in banking changing fast. New services were dreamed up and new divisions created, with impressive-sounding names such as *research and development, human resources, customer relations* and *marketing*. Before long, positions were being advertised in AIB that had never been heard of in its constituent banks, among them that of *public relations manager* (for all of AIB). I applied, and got the job.

In the space of a year, I had been plucked from Mary Street, from the world of ripe bananas, 'Carbery's' chocolate and the last of the dancing monkeys, to an office in Burlington Road and the freedom to define most of the rules myself, a responsibility that I think I can say I accepted gracefully.

There was no time to lose. I called on Aidan O'Hanlon, head of public relations in Bord Failte, one of a group with whom I had enjoyed a winter holiday in Switzerland a few years before. He marked my card and warned me of some of the potential hazards of the job. Thinking this over, I found myself recalling an incident from some years before, when I was preparing to serve my brother at his first Mass. Having little knowledge of the procedures involved (thanks to my aborted career as an altar boy), I was feeling a little nervous that I might make some clumsy mistake on the altar. Ino gave me some astute advice: 'Whatever you do,' he said, 'always make it look afterwards as if it were the right thing, as if it were part of the script.' It struck me that this piece of wisdom might be useful in my new job also. Before I had a chance to put it to the test, however, a second important event took place. On 30 April 1970, the banks went on strike.

With Jimmy Manning (centre) and Tony O'Malley (right), at our first shared exhibition in the Little Theatre in Brown Thomas', 1957.

Mary (centre) at the opening of my exhibition in the premises of the famous Pearl Bar in Fleet Street, shortly after the pub's demise, along with friends, Ciarán MacMathúna and Dolly McMahon.

Following an AIB presentation on the Aran Islands, Angela Cotter and I share a 'taxi' to the airport with *Irish Times* news editor, Donal Foley (front left) and the paper's GAA correspondent, Paddy Downey (right).

The laundrette in London, with its lavish furnishings. When I joined, the team consisted of Tom Moriarty (extreme left) and Gerry O'Mahony (extreme right). Catherine Ryan arrived soon afterwards, while Mick Greally (second left) and Tim Godfrey (second right) followed later. I gave up the pipe years ago, but still occasionally miss it.

From the 1970s, sponsorships became an important part of AIB's promotional activities. Here, *Irish Independent* sports journalist, Raymond Smith (centre) joins me in availing of a visit to Ireland by Muhammed Ali to publicise his book on hurling, sponsored by the bank. Also present were the great Kilkenny hurler, Eddie Keher (left) and Dermot Moloughney, AIB.

The Queen Mother, looking suitably delighted with her AIB plastic money-box, presented to her at the Royal Agricultural Show in Stonely, England by Vincent O'Dea.

I cannot remember the reason for the serious mood of this picture – perhaps it was hearing that I had just two weeks to complete an order for 250 landscape paintings for Pan-American Airways!

The site for *Bankcentre*, AIB's new corporate headquarters in Ballsbridge, was purchased in 1973 for £4.3m. With construction workers after the topping out ceremony were (third from left) AIB chairman, Edmond ('Mon') O'Driscoll; chief executive, Jim Fitzpatrick (third from right); and group chief executive, Joe McGlinn (extreme right).

Bankcentre was officially opened on 19 February 1980 by Charles J. Haughey, then Taoiseach. He is seen here during the ceremony with Niall Crowley, chairman of AIB.

'Big Mac'. This portrait of Brian McCarthy by James Le Jeune was presented to Brian by his friends in Dublin when he was transferred to Killorglin.

Con Howard, legendary diplomat. His creative mind and boundless energy have given us the Merriman Summer School, the St. Brendan Society and the Ireland-Australia Society, among other successful cultural initiatives.

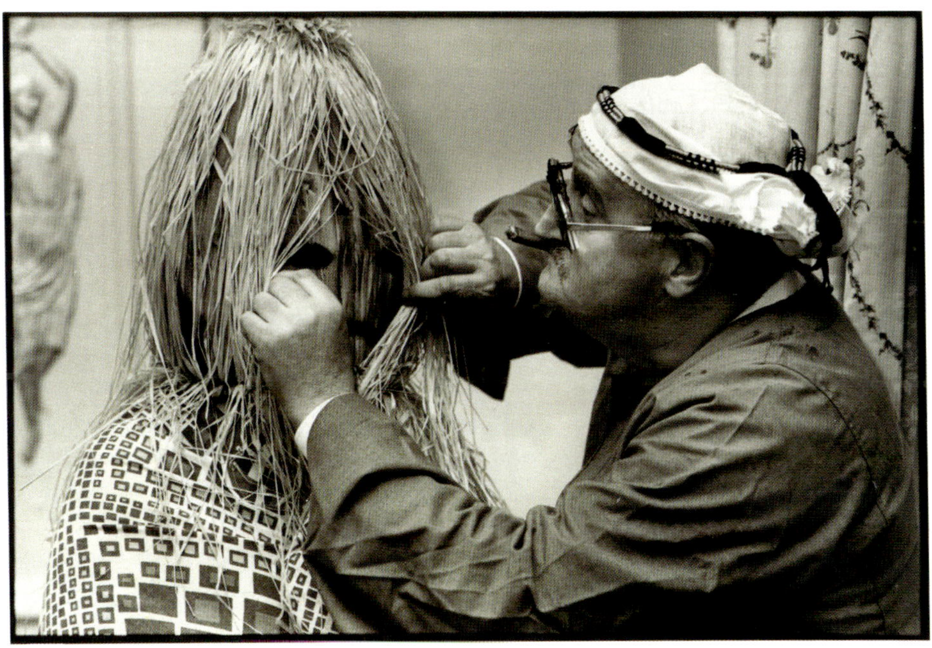

The wran, the wran, the king of all birds. Checking Tom Ahern's disguise for our annual St. Stephen's Day outing. My own is less faithful to tradition.

'The prudent, worthy and far-seeing gentlemen who made up the banking fraternity...' Friends always ask me to identify the faces in this painting, *Bankers*, but none of them was based on any specific individual. They probably reflect my impression of bankers when I first joined the bank, in the days when the N-Nib ruled.

CHAPTER 9

STRIKE

The Irish bank strikes of 1966 and 1970 are worthy of an academic thesis. The 1970 strike in particular was truly remarkable: it is hard to imagine how a country could have survived the complete shutdown of its banking system for more than half a year. I have already mentioned the strength of the IBOA when I entered banking in the late 1940s. A closer look at its history may help to explain how, thirty years later, it managed to achieve virtually unanimous agreement among its members to hold out for almost seven months against the banks and public opinion in pursuit of its demands.

The IBOA was founded in 1917 in the Glentworth Hotel in Limerick (owned, incidentally, by my grandfather). At the time, it had become clear to bank employees that they needed a united front to challenge the paternalistic attitude of the banks and negotiate for better salaries and working conditions. In 1919, the union put before the banks a proposed scale of minimum salaries, starting at eighty pounds per annum and rising to £500 after thirty years service. It also demanded official recognition. The banks vigorously opposed this demand and threatened to lock out staff and bring in volunteer or 'scab' workers from Britain if the union persisted. This was countered by the IBOA, which declared that it would set up a bank in every town in Ireland where staff had been locked out.

The banks reacted swiftly and attempted to undermine the union. They invited handpicked groups of officials to form internal staff associations, with the promise that approaches from these would receive a much more generous response than any likely to be given to the union. It was a decisive moment. Ballots were held. Out of a total poll of 2,437 bank officials, all but ninety-one were against the proposal, deciding instead in favour of strike action. The banks were informed that all officials would cease work on 31 December 1919, with the exception of managers, who normally lived above the branches and would remain on as caretakers.

Pressure to settle the dispute came from a nervous commercial sector, which feared a general bank strike at a difficult time when the country was still trying to cope with the aftermath of the First World War and the 1916 Rising. In the face of this, the banks were forced to accept the IBOA's claim for recognition and agree to arbitration on the proposed salary scale. It was, according to former organising secretary, Job Stott, a most extraordinary development in banking – and not just in Ireland. It set headlines from Britain to South Africa to Australia and New Zealand, and, he maintained (writing on the occasion of the IBOA's seventieth anniversary in 1989) was still influencing the course of industrial relations in banking decades later.

From these revolutionary beginnings developed a union which was always something of an anomaly. Although representing white-collar workers in a sector characterised above all by conservatism, it managed always to retain a surprising militancy and a dogged determination to fight to the end in defence of its principles. Over the years, it also succeeded in attracting and probably developing the skills of many gifted individuals.

One of the foremost of these was John Titterington, who became organising secretary in 1949. A Scotsman, Titterington was not only a fine leader and a skilled negotiator, but also an impressive orator. Job Stott once described him as 'irascible, charismatic and resourceful.' John T., as he was popularly known, was widely rumoured to have been a member of MI5 – and of the Communist Party! In fact, he had led the Scottish Police Association for some years before his appointment to the IBOA. In Ireland, he inspired bankers both north and south of the border (the IBOA had remained an all-Ireland body after partition) to place their hope, trust and total loyalty in him.

As organising secretary, Titterington was employed to carry out the will of the union membership through an executive committee. In reality, he was very much the captain of the ship, although he was blessed in having at his disposal a team of talented committee members drawn from all the associated banks in the country, who fully understood the industry and were in close touch with the aspirations of the union's rank and file. Among those who immediately come to mind were Andy Heffernan, Jim Murray, Jack Gillespie, Harry Dalton, Tom Regan and some very talented women members, including Maureen Collins.

One who particularly stands out for me – and not just because we are friends – was the IBOA's longest-serving honorary secretary, Paddy O'Grady Walshe, a skilled tactician and negotiator who adopted a steely-minded approach to the issues of the moment. He also maintained close contact with members in the branches during the 'quiet' years, when attendances at AGMs fell and the union toiled away on non-salary issues, and he was one of the first to appreciate the importance of the so-called women's vote (the IBOA from its inception had campaigned for equal rights for men and women).

Titterington's skill and the experience of those around him combined to achieve progress in bringing bankers' working conditions up to acceptable levels. Improvements were won painfully over many years through persistent, strenuous negotiations: holidays, an hour's lunch break, overtime pay, a five-day working week, pensions, transfer expenses. Rumblings of discontent seemed to come in roughly four-year cycles, usually when inflation had absorbed whatever advances had been made before. At such times it became difficult to get a seat at meetings in the packed Metropolitan Hall in Abbey Street, where bank managers would cram in side by side with junior staff, all anticipating the organising secretary's report on the latest round of negotiations.

Rising to thunderous applause, Titterington would address the assembly in Churchillian tones. Former broadcaster, Bunny Carr, once an IBOA branch representative in the Bank of Ireland, wrote: 'I sat in awe while his rich Scottish baritone kindled and fanned the desire for change in thousands of ultra-conservative hearts.' By the time he had finished, the members would be straining at the leash, fully behind the executive committee and passing unanimous votes of confidence empowering it to take any reasonable action to achieve its objectives, including, if necessary, the decision to strike. (John O'Shea and I were among those who proposed such action on more than one occasion.)

For a number of years I had the pleasure of sitting on an executive committee with Titterington. It gave me the opportunity to observe at first hand a talented union organiser at work, and to experience the presence of a man of great charm with a wide range of interests, including – of all things – horticulture. He was an acknowledged expert on dahlias, and I will always remember an extremely tense moment during an executive meeting in Belfast, when he suddenly swivelled his chair towards the window, gazed out for a few seconds as if in deep thought, and surprised everyone by calmly remarking that it was ideal weather for planting dahlias. He went on to impart some of the finer points involved in their cultivation, and with this diversion raised a few smiles, lowered the temperature in the room and effortlessly diffused the situation.

This, then, was the cultural background to the 1970 strike. Titterington and the executive confined the dispute to the Republic, but IBOA members in Northern Ireland contributed financial support. The strikers did not receive strike pay, however, and were not entitled to social welfare support. In order to survive, they turned ingeniously to every conceivable type of occupation. Overnight, bank officials became barmen, fishermen, waitresses, labourers, farmhands, secretaries, taxi-drivers, undertakers, book-keepers and dressmakers. A friend of mine, a powerfully built young man named Barney MacBride, took great pleasure in driving a steamroller. Many travelled abroad to work, while some, such as Christy Moore or another friend, Vincent O'Dea, who played a honky-tonk piano in a hotel bar in the Isle of Man, turned a natural talent into a means of earning a living.

In the meantime, the country somehow stumbled on without a banking system. After the initial outcry, people became accustomed to the situation, and many discovered that writing a cheque that could not be cashed was not without its charms. Some, indeed, found their quality of life greatly improved and prayed that the strike might continue indefinitely.

Cheques were written on almost anything that came to hand: pages of children's copybooks, grubby recycled envelopes, the backs of cigarette boxes. All that was required was that the name of the bank, the branch, the amount in words and figures, the signature and the date should appear, with a twopenny postage stamp attached. When the strike finally ended, mountains of these 'cheques' appeared in the banks. A farmer was even rumoured to have presented a cow with all the necessary information scrawled on her hide!

It was a particularly complicated time for the business community, but people soon learned to adapt, and shops, pubs and other businesses cashed and stored away bundles of cheques for future clearance. In some cases these were safely held in respectable safes; in others, they were stashed under mattresses or buried in boxes in back gardens. Towards the end of the dispute the country was beginning to return to the ancient form of payment known as barter, and I remember someone telling me that he saw a motorist trading fresh mackerel for petrol at a garage.

Out of this chaos, strange and sometimes comical situations developed. One concerned a genteel Dublin lady whose accent, *grande dame* manner and a certain eccentricity all contributed to an impression of wealth. The strike was barely a month old when she was struck with some malaise which led her to believe that she had inherited substantial wealth from a dead aunt. Charitable by nature, she decided to allocate much of her inheritance to the needy, her more favoured relatives and various worthy causes. One of her first steps was to visit the prior of a religious order which owned a well-attended church in the city centre, to present him with a cheque for a thousand pounds 'for the missions'. Over tea, they discussed the issues of the day, among them the bank strike. The prior agreed wholeheartedly that it was a dreadful situation. Sighing, his benefactor described her difficulty in obtaining ready cash to donate to charities with immediate needs.

The prior looked thoughtful. 'I might be able to help you there,' he said.

'Really?'

He lowered his voice. 'We do receive quite a...well, a not inconsiderable amount of cash here. In fact, it's a bit of a problem, with the strike. I'm sure we could cash a cheque for you.'

'How awfully kind, Father!' she exclaimed. 'Are you sure?'

'Oh, I think so. How much would you need?'

'Would £2,000 be too much?'

'I think we could manage that.'

She wrote out a cheque for £2,000, and soon he was blessing her and waving her off, her bulging handbag clutched tightly in both hands.

The woman's missions of mercy intensified. Orphanages received new televisions; guide dogs were provided for the blind; relatives found their debts cleared; and when she was hospitalised with a leg injury, the nurses received gifts from an expensive dress shop. Meanwhile, she also found time to visit many other religious orders with surplus cash on their hands.

Around mid-November when the strike was nearing a resolution, the prior chanced to meet the manager of the Grafton Street branch of the bank where he knew his benefactor kept her account. He enquired after her and was surprised when the manager, try as he might, couldn't seem to place her. The following day the prior had an unsettling phone call from the man, in whose mind doubts had been growing. He had done some checking up and discovered that the woman had only a very modest account, just about sufficient to meet her basic needs. He discreetly warned the prior to be careful.

The prior was now a worried man. He nervously rang the woman and invited her to tea. After some chit-chat he got around to mentioning the bank strike, by then on the point of being resolved, and the difficulties the banks were going to have in processing the enormous volume of cheques accumulated over the seven months. Eventually he broached the subject of her donation.

'We were just discussing in the community how generous you have been to us,' he stammered. 'In fact, some of us have been wondering if you haven't been perhaps a little *too* generous. We were wondering whether you – forgive me – whether you can really afford this. Not that I'm worried, of course, but you know what the banks are like. We wouldn't like to be the source of...well, of any difficulties for you.'

The woman laughed heartily. 'Dear Father Prior,' she said, 'I assure you, you have nothing to worry about. However, I understand your concerns. Please don't worry. I'll be back tomorrow, and I'll set your mind at rest.'

The following day she returned with a substantial portion of the cash. Reassured, the prior returned her cheque, which she replaced with a much smaller one for the balance.

It was only when the strike ended that the whole story unravelled. Television sets were reclaimed from orphanages; debts re-surfaced; and religious congregations all over the city, who had unwittingly been involved in a charitable merry-go-round, anxiously began to claim money from one another. For the most part, however, they maintained a holy and embarrassed silence on the affair, and no action was taken against the well-meaning philanthropist.

~

The 1970 strike was a watershed in Irish banking. Bringing it to a successful conclusion took nerve, patience, tenacity and unity of purpose on the part of the IBOA executive and its members. Bank officials emerged with enhanced salaries and better working conditions. The strike set the benchmark for the position of white-collar workers in Ireland for decades, not only in banking but in other sectors also. When it was over, the staff of the banks returned to what can only be described as complete chaos. Without the assistance of computers, they achieved feats in clearing up the mountainous backlog of work that had accumulated over the long closure.

As for me, I cannot say that my role in the affair was a heroic one. I was out of the country for almost the entire seven months.

CHAPTER 10

A LAUNDRETTE IN LONDON

An event occurred in 1966 which must surely stand as one of the great Irish business blunders of the twentieth century. The Bank of Ireland, which had recently acquired the National Bank, sold off the British side of that bank – including some forty branches in prime locations throughout the UK – to the Williams & Glyns Bank in London, for an absurdly low figure.

Established by Daniel O'Connell in 1826, the National Bank was founded in London rather than in Dublin because of the Bank of Ireland's charter, which prevented the opening of any other bank with more than six proprietors within a fifty-mile radius of Dublin. The National was one of the very few designated clearing banks in Britain, with all the rights and privileges implied by that status. Its sale by the Bank of Ireland meant that an important Irish institution in Britain had gone, leaving the door open for an astute competitor to fill the vacuum. Mon O'Driscoll, chairman of AIB, was not one to let such an opportunity pass.

Like the National – and for the same reason – the Provincial Bank had also been founded in London, just two years earlier, in 1824. It too had an interesting history, being one of the first (if not *the* first) joint-stock banks in Britain, meaning that its capital was held in a common fund. After it became absorbed into AIB, the latter bank inherited the prestigious building in London that had once housed the Provincial's Head Office, situated in Throgmorton Avenue under the shadow of the Bank of England, known in banking circles as the 'old lady of Threadneedle Street.'

A few months before the 1970 bank strike began, one of my friends and colleagues in Dame Street, Gerry O'Mahony, was sent to London to research the feasibility of AIB's establishing a branch network in Britain. His reports suggested that such a move would win the support of the Irish community, still somewhat aggrieved by the sale of the National Bank to Williams & Glyns. He was soon joined in London by Tom Moriarty, a noted Kerry footballer of the 1950s, who was despatched from

South Mall in Cork. Much shoe leather was worn out as Gerry and Tom walked the streets of the city looking for an appropriate location for AIB's first branch. They eventually settled on a site on the Kilburn High Road. Pending construction, a temporary office was leased on the Brecknock Corner near Camden, where Brecknock Road crosses the main highway between Camden and Archway. It was not the most sought-after address in London. On one side of the intersection was a pub, imaginatively named 'The Brecknock', while across the road was a recently vacated laundrette and a small cluster of shops. The laundrette became the unlikely launch-pad for AIB's first venture outside Ireland.

Prior to this I had not been greatly aware of these happenings, but just as the strike was about to commence, I was asked to join the London team. It would mean being away from home and the family, but the idea of a few months on foreign territory was exciting. I already had a passing familiarity with London, and I thought it a wonderful city, with its wealth of galleries, museums, concert-halls and theatres.

From a banking point of view, however, it struck me as a curious time to pick for expansion. The strike was about to shut down the banks completely at home, and the outbreak of the Northern Troubles had resulted in a huge political row in which cabinet ministers stood accused of importing arms behind the back of the Taoiseach, Jack Lynch. It didn't seem like the ideal moment for trying to persuade the plain people of Britain (even those with Irish origins) to entrust their money to an Irish bank. I thought of Shakespeare's lines from *Julius Caesar:*

There is a tide in the affairs of men
Which, taken at the flood, leads on to fortune

and mused that in this case the tide looked frankly flat out.

The summer of 1970 in London was one of those rare, warm, golden summers, which began in early spring and lasted well into autumn. In my memory, a heat haze hung over the city for almost the entire year. I arrived fresh off an Aer Lingus flight and went straight to my smart, comfortable hotel in fashionable Kensington, where I found a succinct note from Gerry O'Mahony: *Meet Camden Stores 7.30.*

Camden was one of the best-known Irish enclaves in London. The venue for our meeting turned out to be not a grocery shop but a pub, whose landlady, a widow from Kerry named Liz Mangan, had become kindly disposed to Gerry and Tom. I arrived to find it crowded with dusty, thirsty, strong-looking men from Cork and Kerry, Mayo and Cavan. Dana's Eurovision winner, *All Kinds of Everything*, played endlessly on the juke-box, its butterflies and bees incongruously sandwiched between rousing choruses of *Four Green Fields* and *The Men Behind the Wire*.

It was a long night. When we finally left the Camden Stores, Moriarty persuaded me to accompany him and Gerry to the hotel in Swiss Cottage where they were in residence. I awoke next morning in the spare bed in Moriarty's room, with vague recollections of having arrived at a terrace of Edwardian houses, one of which bore a sign: *Avoca House Hotel*. As dawn broke, I crept out of the room and tiptoed down to the foyer. My head was pounding.

'Morning, sir – can oi 'elp you?'

I jumped. The voice had hit some sensitive place in my brain. 'Eh…no, not at all,' I said, apologetically. 'Sorry to disturb you. I just need some fresh air.'

Feeling weak, I crept in the direction of the door.

'Loverly man, your friend, Mr. Moriarty, loverly man.'

'Eh, yes. Grand man.'

'Oi'm Eric. Oi do noights. Sold Mr. Moriarty a loverly alarm clock the ovver noight. T'rrific toime-keepa. Never fyle, them clocks don't. Need an alarm clock, do you, guv?'

I stared at him blankly, marvelling that anyone could speak so fast so early in the morning. 'Eh…no, not really.'

'Mr. O'Mahony a friend of yours, too, is 'e, sir? Loverly man. See that shirt 'e was wearing last noight? Bought that off o' me, Mr. O'Mahony did. Loverly shirt, that, loverly quality. Got a contact, oi do, in the rag trade, see? Loverly man. Could get you a shirt like that, sir. Yeah. Wouldn't cost you nufink – not loike you'd pye down the market. Sorry, guv, didn't catch your nyme?'

Dazed, I escaped into the street.

The Avoca House, I soon discovered, was a sort of Irish Fawlty Towers owned by a Cavan man who had been persuaded to open an account with the bank and become one of AIB's first customers in London. Loyalty to customers being part of the old banking ethic, Gerry and Tom naturally took up residence there, and I was vigorously exhorted to do likewise without delay. It was goodbye to air-conditioned Kensington.

The Avoca House's décor was straight out of a 1940s black-and-white film melodrama. Chintz curtains, sagging armchairs and greying aspidistras somehow made it seem the perfect setting for a good old-fashioned murder. The Fawlty Towers element was provided by the staff, mostly elderly and of Irish ancestry, apart from Eric, the walnut-faced Cockney who supplemented his income by selling a seemingly limitless range of merchandise to the guests. Its character was completed by the curious assortment of slightly dotty patrons who seemed to be in permanent residence there.

Later that morning, we made our way to the laundrette on the Brecknock Corner. A sign over the door indicated that it was now an Allied Irish Banks representative office, and for the sake of the uninitiated, the names of the Munster & Leinster, the Provincial and the Royal were included. The washing machines were gone, but the place was devoid of any adornment. The main room and a small anteroom together provided just enough space for a couple of desks, four chairs, a telephone and a typewriter. Upstairs there was a toilet and a kitchen, with some chipped crockery and a greasy gas stove.

Not quite knowing what to do, I sat down and took a pen in hand, vaguely reflecting on my role in this great undertaking. I found myself thinking ahead to our first press release. *Allied Irish Banks opens first office outside Ireland*, I wrote with a flourish. I looked around the office. It was hard to think what to write next.

Our team of three was soon augmented by a welcome addition, Catherine Ryan, who had previously been secretary to Tom Casey, manager of South Mall in Cork. Like many another bank official during the strike, she had come to London in search of work, and now found herself unexpectedly re-employed by AIB under very different circumstances, far from the grandeur of 66 South Mall. She was paid from the petty cash, which was fuelled on occasion by a loan from an obliging Cockney butcher across the road. As well as efficiently taking care of the administration of the office, she was also a talented cook who would sometimes perform culinary feats for us with the butcher's best beef on the battered old stove upstairs.

The actor, T. P. McKenna, lived nearby and became a regular visitor. He would drop in for coffee in the mornings and entertain us with hilarious yarns of his experiences in the theatre and in films, or during his time with the Ulster Bank. I suspect that it was to him that the laundrette's nickname, *Hangover Creek*, can be traced: he was a frequent witness to the toll taken by the after-hours promotional activities engaged in by the inhabitants of the laundrette on behalf of the bank.

Thanks to a largely preoccupied AIB executive in Dublin, we had been left more or less to our own devices, out of sight and mind of Head Office. We didn't complain. With hindsight, it turned out to be fortuitous from the bank's point of view also, for it left Gerry and Tom free to read the situation on the ground and adopt what they saw as the best approach to the job in hand. Their methods may have been somewhat unorthodox, but they produced the desired results. The basic task was to find customers for the bank, and the main target, initially, at least, was the Irish community. No banker with a briefcase was going to cut any ice with a successful builder by arriving on a site in the middle of a sunny afternoon, and publicans were not interested in discussing interest rates while pulling pints or trying to deal with the man from the brewery. And so, as in the Percy French ballad, we found ourselves working literally 'by day and by night'.

Thanks to his heroic deeds on the football pitch, Tom Moriarty had the support of many GAA friends in London, and through them, he gained access to a seemingly unending network of potential customers. Doors firmly closed to others sprang miraculously open for Tom, who, as well as having a warm and sociable nature, inspired people with complete confidence in his integrity. Tom's great love of sport extended even to that most un-Irish of sports, cricket, for which he had a deep appreciation. He once persuaded me to accompany him to Lords to see the great West Indian cricketer, Gary Sobers. As we sat at the Tavern end of the ground sipping pints of warm brown ale, he turned to me and said, with some awe in his voice, 'Ye know – 'tis hard to believe, but this is their Croke Park!'

Tom's style of operation on the job was unique. One evening I set out with him to visit a pub in North London, where one of his GAA contacts had arranged a meeting with the Irish landlord. We began with the usual ritual of paying our respects to the Widow Mangan, before heading off in a taxi for the outskirts of the city. At our destination, formal introductions were followed by a rambling conversation revolving mainly around hurling, Arsenal's chances in the Cup and tips for the dogs at White City.

Banking, or the reason for our visit, was never mentioned.

When closing time came and the house was cleared, the landlord threw a towel over the taps and invited us to join him in his flat upstairs.

'Daly tells me you're opening a bank in Kilburn?' he remarked nonchalantly.

'At the end of the year, please God,' Tom replied.

'Could I open an account now?'

'No problem. We'll keep it in Throgmorton Avenue down in the City for the time being.'

The landlord opened a safe, brought out a suitcase, produced a bottle of whiskey and filled three tumblers. 'Check that,' he said casually, nodding at the suitcase. 'There should be around £60,000 in it.'

'Grand,' said Tom.

We drank the whiskey and counted the notes. Dawn was lighting up the chimney pots as we returned to the hotel in a taxi, brown paper bags stuffed with notes on our knees. Arriving at the Avoca House, we ordered a couple of celebratory glasses from Eric, the night porter, and stowed the paper bags under Moriarty's bed, awaiting their transfer to Throgmorton Avenue.

Many accounts were opened in this manner. On one occasion, arriving by taxi at the laundrette in the morning after a night spent similarly to the one above (although with a somewhat less prosperous client), we discovered that we had left the bag with the night's booty on the back seat of the taxi. It contained several thousand pounds, and we spent an anxious morning wondering how the bank might react to the news. Fortunately, the honest cabbie went to the police, who tracked us down with a business card of Moriarty's discovered among the banknotes. A phone call from the police-station smoothed our furrowed brows, and our regard for London taxi-drivers soared.

As the laundrette was only a representative office, it did not indulge in normal day-to-day banking transactions. Lodgments of cash taken in late-night forays had to be deposited in the Provincial Bank's former Head Office in Thorgmorton Avenue. This, tucked in among the giants of international finance in the City, was a relic from another era. Its small public office had a carved, polished mahogany counter, over which a large ticking clock measured out the seconds at what felt like a particularly sedate pace. The occasional creaking of the main door announced the entrance of a splendidly top-hatted porter from the Bank of England, bearing a communication for the manager. Rummaging in a dusty back room there one day, I came across a cobwebbed cardboard box containing some yellowed correspondence that included a letter from Charles Dickens.

Apart from a few wealthy merchants, it seemed that only directors of the bank and some very senior business executives were deemed worthy to open an account with the Provincial at Throgmorton Avenue. The silver-haired manager, Harold Clarke, was the quintessential English bank manager from an age long gone. Reserved and precise, he wore bespoke suits of impeccable tailoring and highly-polished shoes. His knowledge of Irish history and culture seemed slight, and I suspect that he viewed AIB with a jaundiced eye. The culture of the Royal Bank he might have understood; that of the Munster & Leinster would undoubtedly have sent shudders down his spine. His relationship with Gerry O'Mahony was nonetheless cordial, and they managed to communicate. Tom Moriarty from the Dingle peninsula, with his All-Ireland medals, was a different proposition – and the feeling was mutual. To Clarke, Tom might have just emerged from the Australian bush country beyond Toorawoomba, wearing a loincloth and carrying a didgeridoo; to Moriarty, Clarke could have been a Saxon elder. Not even sign language could bridge the gap between them.

Once, after one of his nightly excursions, Tom Moriarty had opened an account for an Irish building contractor who was preparing the foundations for the new London Stock Exchange, just around the corner from the branch in Throgmorton Avenue. The project involved hundreds of workers, almost all of them Irish. Tom had converted the contractor to the idea of paying them by cheque rather than in cash, which was his usual practice. This would lessen the secretarial workload and encourage the workers to save some of their wages in Clarke's branch, where they would be encouraged to go to cash their cheques.

The following Friday afternoon, I happened to be in the branch at Throgmorton Avenue. It was a day of humid, almost tropical heat. Suddenly the door burst open and an army of heavily sweating men pounded in, shattering the silence. Bare to the waist or wearing grimy singlets, in dust-covered trousers, boots and yellow helmets, they looked almost menacing as they surveyed the bank with expressions of mistrust. The assistant manager, Victor Grosse, arose from his desk and straightened himself up to his full height. He was (in spite of the name) a tall thin man, much in the Clarke mould, who would not have been out of place at a garden party in Buckingham Palace.

'I say,' he demanded imperiously, 'what are you doing here? What do you want?'

'Cash for this effin' cheque,' growled a voice from west of the Shannon, brandishing a piece of paper in the air like a weapon.

Grosse frowned. 'Cheque? Let me see.' He stretched an elegant arm towards the mob. Several cheques were waved under his nose. He took one delicately and looked at it. His frown deepened. 'I have absolutely no authority to cash this cheque,' he declared in firm tones.

'Listen, son, this is where we were told to come. An' we've got betther things to be doin' than hangin' around here all day with our tongues hangin' out with the thirst.' He turned to the terrifying-looking giant standing next to him. 'Amn't I right there, Pa?'

'Pa' obliged with a growl of assent.

Hearing the commotion, Clarke emerged from his office.

'What on earth is going on here, Grosse?' he enquired. 'Who are these men?'

'They appear to have cheques drawn on us, Manager.'

Clarke surveyed the scene with distaste.

'Nonsense,' he said. 'There has obviously been a mistake. Perhaps they've been misdirected. Take care of it, Grosse. Get them out of here.' He turned on his heel and returned to his office, clicking on a red light to indicate that he was not to be disturbed.

Left alone to deal with the situation, Grosse called for reinforcements and was joined by two nervous-looking assistants. As if deciding to start afresh, he took the cheque again from the man before him and this time studied it more carefully.

'P. J. Bourke,' he read aloud, prounouncing it 'Boorke'. 'But how am I to know if you are P. J. Boorke? Have you got any form of identification?'

'Lookit,' roared Bourke, 'why would I have his cheque if I wasn't him? Who the hell else would I be? Ask them!' A sweep of his arm indicated his fellow-workers. 'Sure, anyone'll tell ye. Now, will ye cash the cheque an' let me bloody-well outa here before I....'

Becoming thirsty myself – the heat in the office had suddenly become unbearable – I squeezed my way to the door and left them to it.

To keep ourselves afloat financially in the laundrette, we were permitted to open temporary personal accounts in Throgmorton Avenue. We were expected to submit records of expenses – receipts and the like – to Dublin at regular intervals, and money from Head Office would be lodged to our accounts to wipe out any overdraft that might have built up. Alas, paperwork and managing expenses were not among my strengths. Keeping an eagle eye on casual overdrafts, on the other hand, was a particular talent of Harold Clarke's. After several weeks in London, my expenses had still not come through from Dublin and my account was well overdrawn. One day, I received an agitated phone-call from Clarke.

'Ryan! Clarke speaking. Something dreadful has happened. Can't speak on the telephone. Can you come down here immediately?'

In his office, he invited me to take a chair. On the desk in front of him was a pile of cheques which I immediately recognised as my own. Gravely, Clarke began to explain that among the accounts held at the branch was one in the name of a director of the bank, one Walter Mary Ryan, by all accounts a sober, upright citizen who lived a quiet and God-fearing life at a respectable address in Dublin. By some quirk, my signature was almost identical to his, and since my arrival in London, the branch at Throgmorton Avenue had been posting large numbers of my cheques to his account. Perusing his paid cheques returned by the bank one day, he was startled to notice that many had been made out to establishments unfamiliar to him: The King and Keys, The Red Lion, The Camden Stores. Stranger still were the number made out simply to *Cash*. He had contacted the bank, and Clarke, in a state of shock, had apologised profusely. Realising there had been a mistake, he assured him that his account would be credited for the various amounts immediately.

'I hope he didn't get too much of a shock,' I said politely.

'Indeed. However, Ryan, if I may come to the nub of the matter. While we have refunded Mr. Ryan, the fact is that we now have to post these cheques to your account.'

'Of course you do,' I said agreeably. 'That's fine. Go ahead.'

Clarke's expression turned even graver than usual.

'Well, not quite, Mr. Ryan. You may not be aware of it, but your account is already seriously overdrawn – against *all* standing instructions on staff accounts, may I say. In fact, the seriousness of the situation is such that if we were to post those cheques to your account now, it would…well, frankly, it would be completely *out of control*. A matter for Head Office! Furthermore, it would also highlight the kind of places (his nose quivered slightly) that you…you people…seem to be frequenting.'

I tried to explain about the bank strike in Ireland which was greatly disrupting the efficiency with which things were being handled in Dublin. I tried to reassure him that all my expenses *would* eventually come through, and that all would be well. I also tried to enlighten him as to the purpose of our mission in London, and the role of public relations, and to impress upon him the importance to AIB of contacts such as the Widow Mangan, or P. J. Bourke's boss, or the journalists who were the London correspondents of the Irish newspapers. At the mention of journalists, a look of such horror came over his face that I threw in the towel. I left with assurances that I would sort out my account, promising that I would try to do better in future.

CHAPTER 11

ON GRUB STREET

By 1970, the Irish in Britain – particularly if one included a second generation – had begun to play important roles in many areas of public life, including industry, business, education, medicine and the world of entertainment. Irish success in the construction industry was already well established. I remember once meeting a successful builder who handed me a business card with the letters 'F.L.C.' added after his name. The 'F' I took to stand for 'Fellow'; the 'C' might relate to 'construction', but the 'L' was a puzzle. I later asked a friend of the builder's if he knew what the letters meant. '*Failed Leaving Certificate*,' he replied!

The media was another area where an Irish presence was beginning to be felt. There were, of course, publications specifically targeted at the Irish community, such as the *Irish Post*, which first appeared around the time I arrived in London, with Breandain MacLua, former Irish-language editor of the Irish Press, as its managing editor. A special London weekly edition of the *Cork Examiner* detailed Irish sporting and social events in London and beyond, and I was also surprised at the range and quantity of Irish provincial newspapers sold outside Catholic churches after Sunday Mass and on news-stands throughout the city.

In the brief period that had elapsed between my entrance into public relations in Dublin and my departure for London, the importance of gaining the confidence of the media had been firmly impressed upon me. Transferred to London, I relished the prospect of getting to know the legendary Fleet Street and the characters reputed to frequent its various pubs and restaurants. At the time, 'Grub Street', as it was known, was the centre of gravity not only of the main British newspapers, both broadsheets and tabloids, but also for the London correspondents of much of the foreign press, including Ireland's. It was time to introduce myself.

Perhaps some subliminal Cork influence was at work when I decided that my first call would be on James Whelan, London editor of the *Cork Examiner*. Whelan had been in Fleet Street for longer than most people could remember. By now elderly and somewhat frail, in his winged and starched collar he looked very much the gentleman journalist from another time, but he was still keenly alert. Preliminary introductions over, I invited him to lunch at a restaurant, Ye Olde Cocke Tavern, a short distance from his office. As we chatted over grilled turbot and a glass of wine, he quizzed me and took notes on AIB and its activities in London.

A few days later, I glanced at a copy of the *Examiner* and was pleased to see that he had made our conversation the subject of his London column. It was good publicity for the bank, and I made a point of calling to his office to thank him. I was met at the door by a man with a handlebar moustache, who might have just stepped out of the cockpit of an RAF Spitfire.

'I say,' he exclaimed, recognising me, 'aren't you the chap who took Whelan to lunch the other day?'

'That's right,' I said. 'Is he in? Could I have a word with him?'

He shook his head sadly. 'I'm afraid he's in Guy's Hospital, poor chap. Believe he's very poorly. Bad case of food poisoning apparently. Delicate tummy, our Mr. Whelan – doesn't normally eat much. I'm afraid something went badly against him.'

I wandered down Fleet Street feeling deflated, reflecting that I would have to be more careful in future. It was surely not in the manual of public relations to poison one's first London editor.

Further down the street was the office of the *Irish Press*. Climbing the stairs and entering a chaotic newsroom, I saw a well-rounded figure in shirtsleeves behind a desk, with an agreeable, jovial appearance. Broad braces held up his trousers; a phone rested beneath his chin. There were untidy bundles of old newspapers piled up on the floor behind him and a half-empty mug teetered on the edge of the desk. He seemed to be in the middle of a heated discussion, which he interrupted to mouth a question at me.

'Can I help you? Are you looking for someone?'

'I was wondering if I could speak to Aidan Hennigan?' I asked. (Hennigan was the paper's London editor.)

'This is he!' He slammed the phone down. 'Can you believe it?' he declared with an air of exasperation. 'Those subs in Burgh Quay have managed to leave out a paragraph that was absolutely vital. Again!' He shook his head with an air of long sufferance, then shrugged it off as if deciding it wasn't worth bothering about, and turned his full attention to me.

'So – what can I do for you, then? Would you like a cup of coffee?'

Thus began a friendship with the doyen of the Irish press corps in London. Aidan Hennigan's views on anything relating to life in London or elsewhere in Britain – as, indeed, on most things – were always worth noting. Generous, hospitable and hugely humorous, he could find amusement in even the most calamitous situation.

I would occasionally eschew the delights of the Avoca House to spend a night in his ground-floor flat in one of the charming little side streets of Chelsea. On one such occasion, he had misplaced his spare key and told me (since it looked like it might be a long night) that he would leave the front window open so that I could let myself in. Returning in the early hours, I located the window, lifted it as quietly as I could and climbed into the room, which was in total darkness. I was just about to pull the sash back down when I was startled by the sound of an unfamiliar male voice.

'That you, Ethel?' it asked, with a hint of anxiety.

I froze. The voice seemed to come from within feet of where I stood. There was a sound as of someone turning over, followed by a sleepy, slightly grumpy reply. 'Hmm? Is what me?'

A moment's silence.

'I thought I heard something. Sshhh…'

Rooted to the floorboards, I realised that I was in the wrong house. I could either throw myself at their feet, declare my mistake and beg for mercy…or I could run for it. Going with a basic survival instinct, I hurled myself back through the window, colliding noisily with a collection of dustbins, and fled up the street as fast as I could. Aidan derived much merriment from this story over breakfast the following morning, his large tomcat, Carruthers (who didn't like strangers), draped across his knee and eyeing me coldly.

Across the road from the *Irish Press* and beside the offices of the *Daily Telegraph* stood The King and Keys, gathering place for the London-based Irish media and visiting Irish journalists, as well as for the occasional Irish politician or other public figure passing through the British capital. Its landlord, a Limerick man named Mark O'Donnell, had a reputation on Fleet Street as a generous and well-liked guv'nor, and the pub had also become popular with journalists from the *Daily Telegraph, Daily Express, Daily Mail* and other Fleet Street publications. The King and Keys was a clearing-house for every conceivable type of information, gossip, rumour and intrigue. It was there that I was surprised to learn one day that news of our little laundrette and its activities had spread far wider than I could ever have thought possible.

The source of this information was a Dubliner, Gerry Lawless, a freelance journalist based in London whose lively imagination, quick sense of humour and alert, suspicious mind was matched by bobbing and weaving movements that always reminded me of a canny lightweight boxer. On this occasion, he drew me aside with dark hints of having something important and confidential to reveal. We retreated to a corner. Gerry cut to the point.

'Yis'r been followed,' he announced.

'What? Who? What do you mean, Gerry?'

'The bank. The laund-er-ette (he pronounced it deliberately, with three syllables). They're onta yis.'

'What are you talking about?'

'The Special Branch – British,' he whispered, out of the corner of his mouth. 'They're followin' yis!'

'Ah, come on!' It was too absurd not to be a joke. 'How do you know?'

'Contacts. Cheltenham Centre. They figure yis are up to somethin' in that laund-er-ette.'

'Are you serious?'

'True as I'm standin' here. They reckon yis'r after money for the boys. Keep yer eyes open and ye'll soon see. Yis'r been followed day and night. Say nuthin' – here comes Hennigan.'

I tried to follow his advice, and for a couple of days imagined that everyone who crossed my path dressed in a raincoat with a turned-up collar was probably MI5. After that, I forgot about it. Later, Gerry O'Mahony confirmed through a reliable source that my informant had not been exaggerating.

Gerry Lawless was the archetypical northside 'Dub'. He was slight of frame and had a badly damaged eye resulting from an altercation with the forces of the law in Dublin. He had been incarcerated for political activities for a brief period, and had the distinction of being the first Irish citizen to challenge and succeed in a case taken against the Irish state in the European Courts of Justice.

Remembering him, I am carried forward to another incident which took place a couple of years later. My residential internship in London finished at the end of 1970, but I continued to pay frequent visits thereafter while the bank was establishing itself in Britain. On the morning after Bloody Sunday in Derry, I was having coffee in The King and Keys with Catherine Ryan, who was then working in Throgmorton Avenue. The mood among the Irish in the pub was one of anger and disbelief. Suddenly Gerry appeared, bristling all over. In camouflage battledress, he was all business. He had come to round up people to join in a protest march from Hyde Park Corner to Downing Street. Like everyone else, Catherine and I were full of indignation at the events of the day before, and it didn't take much to persuade us.

A large crowd had gathered at Hyde Park Corner. Catherine and I were marshalled into position by Gerry near the front of the parade, a step or two ahead of a large banner and immediately behind thirteen black coffins which were to be carried in protest to Downing Street. Our respectable business attire looked decidedly out of place against what seemed to be the standard dress code: khaki battle outfits, blue denim, long hair and tee-shirts decorated with badges in support of various anti-establishment causes. I began to feel conspicuous.

The signal was given and the march set off. We proceeded down Park Lane behind the coffins, policemen lining both sides of the route. Television cameras and press photographers seemed to be everywhere. I had a sudden mental picture of AIB senior executives back in Dublin settling down to watch the evening news. Uneasily, I took a few steps forward to glance up at the banner under which we were marching. *The Communist Party of Great Britain supports the IRA,* it read. Almost involuntarily, I found myself bending slightly at the knees in an absurd attempt to reduce my height and appear less visible. It was no use. Gerry Lawless, meanwhile, armed with a megaphone, continued to rally the protesters, leading the chants and delivering a blaring commentary on what was going on. His eye lit on me, and perhaps recognising a potential defector, he bellowed into his megaphone before the assembled TV cameras: *'And we have Bob Ryan of the AIB here! The bourgeoisie are off their ass at last!'*

Recalling my brother's advice of years before ('Whatever you do, always make it look as if it were the right thing'), I found myself thinking grimly that this was going to take some explaining if the bank should get wind of it.

~

The bank strike ended in November. On 7 December 1970, AIB's first branch in Britain was officially opened in Kilburn. An official lunch to mark the event took place in the Hilton in Park Lane, but the real celebration was held not in the City nor in the premises of the Institute of Directors, but in Tommy O'Gorman's Ballroom in Archway. It was, as they say, a hooley and a half, with a guest list that included diplomats and plumbers, publicans and dentists, actors, builders and newspaper hacks – and the proprietor of a hotel called the Avoca House.

Tom Moriarty returned home, eventually to become AIB's general manager for the West of Ireland, while Gerry O'Mahony took up the post of general manager in Britain, where he rapidly built up a thriving Irish bank. From the humble and slightly ramshackle beginnings described here, AIB went on to forge a new destiny as a successful international financial services company.

I got back to Dublin just in time for Christmas.

CHAPTER 12

PRESSING CONCERNS

With the bank strike finally resolved and the expansion of AIB into Britain under way, the changes that had begun with the amalgamation of three banks into one gathered pace. The old order was slipping away into the shadows, in some cases as imperceptibly as an autumn leaf carried by the wind; in others amid creaks and groans of protest.

Bucolic old managers who had made an art out of lending money only to those who could prove conclusively that they did not really need it, suddenly found themselves faced with over-confident young whipper-snappers who flummoxed them with talk of rationalisation, new methods of operation, open door policies and targets. Worse of all was their familiar manner and their pretence of seeking an opinion on matters that invariably turned out to have already been decided elsewhere. 'John!' they would begin warmly, with a vigorous handclasp. 'Good to meet you! How're you doing? I'm Frank Speed – call me Frankie. I'm from Development. Look, I'd like to run a few ideas past you – got a minute?'

These characters were despised by many of the older generation of bankers, accustomed to being addressed as *Mr. Meehan*, *Manager* or *Sir*. They muttered darkly about the consequences of bringing in outsiders who knew nothing about banking, but even as their doom-laden prophesies were being uttered, new names and faces continued to appear – sometimes in senior positions, sometimes under the magic catch-all of 'consultant'. There was no stopping the unstoppable force.

One of the early forerunners of change – an expert in something or other – arrived from a leading London bank with what was said to be a clever scheme that would enable bank managers to capitalise on key business opportunities. Managers were brought together to attend presentations held at different locations around the country, where the plan was unveiled with the aid of an impressive array of slides, overhead projectors and other paraphernalia to which we had not been much exposed before. It all felt very modern.

The project was code-named KBI, which stood for 'Key Business Influencers'. KBIs, we learned, could be the springboard to an ocean of new business for the bank. It was already out there, waiting to be harvested. And who were these KBIs? Where were they to be found? Why, everywhere, apparently: it was simply a matter of recognising them. This information was delivered like the divine revelation of some deity devoted to corporate business development.

'A KBI,' the expert droned, 'can sometimes be found in the most unexpected places. Naturally, you will find them in politics, in the civil service and in big business. However, the question we must ask is this: who influences the influencers?' His audience gasped on cue at this fascinating thought. The answer, we learned, included not only trade union representatives, local councillors and gardaí, but also ICA members, schoolteachers, the wives of men of power – perhaps even taxi-drivers, with their definite views on most things.

'The chap you play golf with, for example. Did you ever think that *he* might be a Key Business Influencer? Who else can you think of?'

'What about a mistress?' came a muffled voice from the back row.

'Would a poet qualify?' someone else asked, producing a glazed look on the face of the expert from London.

As the talk proceeded, it emerged that the bank's plan was to allow – nay, to encourage – managers to seek out these people, nurture them and even spend money if necessary on entertaining them, wooing them and generally conveying the impression that their business would be valued by the bank. It was, in other words, a complete reversal of the attitude of the past.

Over the following few years, KBIs were hunted down relentlessly. Expense accounts were opened in the branches and managers sallied forth, armed with chequebooks. Some were entirely sceptical, but others discovered a talent for wining and dining, warmed to their new role and were soon identifying KBIs daily – in some cases, it was rumoured, even among their relatives and friends. More conscientious managers lay awake at night, fretful about the responsibility of it all. Several things were worrying them. It had been explained that a KBI might well be identified among the bank's existing account-holders, but what if the likely suspect had some sticky debts with the bank? And what if hundred of pounds were spent on someone who turned out to be a *non*-KBI? It was an alarming thought. Small wonder that some of those targeted were bewildered by the new warmth and solicitude suddenly visited upon them.

Operation KBI became the butt of many a joke, but it probably did serve a purpose in luring down from their ivory towers certain managers who might have clung forever to the traditions of the past. Also, in fairness, the new breed of banker – the experts who were parachuted in among us from other worlds – included men of indisputable talent who made a major contribution to a necessary process of change.

Among these was Brian Whelan, an experienced consultant in strategic management. His task was to put in place a regional structure and to develop within it the skills necessary to enable AIB to consolidate its business and ensure growth. He was closely supported in this by the bank's chief executive, Joe McGlinn, along with others who understood the need to overhaul the diverse systems that persisted within AIB even after the merger. Whelan had the sensitivity to appreciate the values inherited from the past, and he understood the pressures of in-house political manoeuvring. The structures he put in place were central to the bank's phenomenal development over the following decades. The fact that he also displayed a keen social conscience added another dimension to all his dealings. It was perhaps predictable that this would eventually result in tensions. Regrettably for the bank, Brian left to pursue his wider interests and channel his skills towards developmental issues in the Third World.

One of the biggest changes to affect banking around this time was the arrival of the accountancy professional. This heralded the beginning of the end of the old-style career banker, who joined the bank straight from school and was promoted over time from clerk to cashier to accountant (assistant manager), eventually achieving the ultimate goal of becoming manager of a branch. Familiar at first hand with every aspect of the practice and law of banking, these men often dealt extremely capably with a very wide range of banking and management issues, but formal education was becoming more important and the trend towards specialisation was beginning to affect every profession and business.

As for me, my job in public relations was also being shaped

by the pace of developments around me: in the bank, on the one hand, and in society in general on the other. By the 1970s, the impact of television was beginning to show in Ireland, easing in changes which in turn were reflected back by the print media, previously inclined to be circumspect and fairly docile. In private, many journalists held strong, unblinkered, perhaps even radical views, but in print, the country's numerous sacred cows had long been left to graze unmolested. Now, on television programmes such as *The Late, Late Show*, we watched spellbound as interviewers dared address ministers, bishops and other dignitaries face to face, sometimes openly challenging them. We saw how ordinary – even how vulnerable – the nation's leaders could appear, and to sense a hollowness behind some of their declarations that at times bordered on the hilarious.

Once again, journalists became central to my working life. Bankers have one thing in common with journalists: they both need to have a keen nose for news and information, and a sense of curiosity about the world about them. In the past, however, the media in Ireland had shown little interest in the banks other than in the specialised context of the financial pages, while the banks had seen themselves as outside (and probably above) the world of journalism. Now, with awareness growing of the role of Mammon in affairs of state, the media was becoming more watchful. The newly formed AIB was an obvious target for its attention. It seemed obvious to me that the bank would have to recognise this and adjust its attitude to accommodate the new reality. Common sense suggested that it was important to try and build a climate of mutual trust.

From the media's point of view, bankers often totally failed to grasp the all-important concept of newsworthiness. Extensions to branches, minor appointments or the latest marketing initiative were not the stuff of headlines. In my early years in public relations, I remember inviting a *Cork Examiner* reporter to the opening of a branch in Blackpool, only to be told with some exasperation that Blackpool needed a brothel more than a bank.

Another of my first lessons in news value – not to mention timing – came when I sent a press release announcing a new appointment in the bank to one of the national dailies, accompanied by a photograph. It landed on the desk of a picture editor who, that very day, had had a cheque bounced by the bank. In the photograph that appeared in the paper the following morning, the executive in question had mysteriously mutated into a blood-sucking vampire, subtle alterations to the picture making his teeth look as though they had been filed down to resemble fangs.

On another occasion, I received a phone-call from a top photographer with a daily newspaper, a man with whom I had spent a considerable amount of time (not to mention the bank's money) 'networking'. We had in fact become good friends.

'Bob,' he asked in an urgent tone of voice, 'is there any chance you can get me out of here?'

'Where are you?'

'I'm in Mountjoy Jail,' came the unexpected reply.

'What are you doing there?' I asked, assuming he was on some special assignment.

'You bastards have put me here,' he declared, with some feeling, 'and all for the sake of a few hundred quid!'

~

There were some in AIB who were quick to appreciate the growing power of the media. The chairman of the bank, Mon O'Driscoll, was not generally thought of as a good public speaker (partly because he was nearsighted and read speeches with difficulty) but he certainly had an instinct for communications. At a press conference held in London in 1974, O'Driscoll took not only the assembled journalists but even the entire board and executive of the bank completely by surprise.

We had a custom in the bank of sometimes running through a sort of dress rehearsal for press conferences earlier in the day or the evening before. My colleague, Angela Cotter, and I, along with some senior managers, would play the role of journalists and fire likely questions at the team assembled on the platform, giving them a foretaste of what was to come and ensuring they were well prepared.

The press conference at which O'Driscoll dropped his bombshell had been arranged to mark the celebration of the 150th anniversary of the founding of the Provincial Bank in London. Over drinks in The King and Keys the night before, Gerald Luke, economics correspondent with the London office of the Press Association, had asked me whether the bank, which was prospering in Britain, had any plans for expansion into the US. I didn't think so, but it was an interesting question and I raised it at the 'dummy run' of the press conference the following morning. The answer was a definite no: AIB would continue to focus its expansion on the UK market.

The press conference proper took place later that day. Gerald Luke was present, and he asked the question again. To the utter astonishment of everyone, Mon O'Driscoll responded without hesitation by announcing AIB's immediate expansion into a number of key cities in America and, for good measure, into Europe. The jaws of some of the bank's own executives were seen to drop open at this news. The unexpected announcement received substantial press coverage the following day, particularly in the Irish papers. There could be no going back: the bank was now committed to expanding abroad. It was game, set and match to O'Driscoll.

The bank's most effective communicator with the media, however, was probably Joe McGlinn, chief executive of the AIB group. Late of the Munster & Leinster, 'Honest Joe', as he was known, was a remarkably intelligent banker and a gentleman in every sense of the word. He was also one of those rare senior executives who made life easy for those of us responsible for the bank's day-to-day relationship with the media.

Joe McGlinn's instincts, or perhaps his innate integrity, led him to take journalists into his confidence and in some cases even to allow them access to privileged information, so as to give them a better understanding of the background to a particular decision. Because of this, I suspect there may have been times when the financial correspondents had more inside information on contentious banking issues than many of the bank's own senior managers. Journalists appreciated McGlinn's openness, and to the best of my knowledge, no one ever broke the confidential nature of such briefings.

~

Meeting journalists on their own ground ironically meant that I once again found myself spending a lot of time in pubs – I say 'ironically' because of the banks' traditional disapproval of staff frequenting such places. The banks' attitude to the licensed trade was always somewhat ambivalent, however. Although many of the staff of the Munster & Leinster were the sons and daughters of publicans, alcohol, known to have a loosening effect on the tongue, was certainly frowned upon.

On the other hand, in the nineteenth century, when the famous Franciscan monk, Fr. Mathew, was traversing the country persuading great numbers of people to 'take the pledge', the banks became positively alarmed at the outbreak of temperance. At its Annual General Meeting in 1840, the directors of the Provincial Bank reported that the crusade against drink was '*paralysing to a great degree the business of Distillers and Brewers...putting an end to the trade of many who gained a living as publicans.*' This drive to temperance was described as being 'productive of much distress', and – getting to the nub of the matter, one suspects – was judged to '*operate injuriously against the regular payment of bills*'. (The banks have always been big lenders to the highly profitable licensed trade.)

I soon discovered that journalists seemed to favour exactly the type of pub I myself preferred. In swirls of tobacco smoke in the dark recesses of Mulligan's, Bowes' and later, Doheny & Nesbitt's, I listened and learned and came to a better understanding of the pressures that journalists work under: the deadlines, the constraints on space in column inches, the competition to get in first with a good story and the short attention-span of the public. I enjoyed the convivial atmosphere, the appetite for talk and the good humour that seemed to pervade these places.

I had no sooner got back from London than the banks began to hit the front pages as armed robbery became a regular occurrence, often masterminded by paramilitary organisations. It was a time when banks staffs were held at gunpoint and security vans hijacked, when managers and sometimes their families might be kidnapped and held to ransom.

My first assignment on my return to Dublin, indeed, was a stormy press briefing in a branch on Arran Quay – a traumatic event, since it involved the death of a member of the gardaí, Garda Fallon, who had been shot on the premises. This was followed by a raid by the Littlejohn brothers on a branch (previously of the Royal Bank) in Grafton Street. Staff arriving for work were locked in the vaults by the raiders, who then forced the porter at gunpoint to make tea for themselves and the imprisoned staff. The urbane and unfailingly courteous manager, Noel Curran, calmly smoked his pipe as he attempted to debate some abstract moral point related to robbery with the raiders.

While all of this was naturally a matter of extreme concern, bank raids were not always without their humorous moments. One in particular, which was not reported in the media, had all the elements of a Keystone Cops film. It began when armed men raided an AIB branch in Killarney. Before being clubbed over the head with a handgun, the assistant manager, Noel Long, managed to press an alarm button connected to the local garda station. A special unit of the gardaí, armed for such emergencies, sprang into action. Fearing a shoot-out, they cleared the streets in the vicinity, surrounded the bank and called on the gang with loud-hailers to come out with their hands up. They didn't realise that the bank they were besieging was occupied only by bewildered customers and staff, frozen with fear. The raiders, meanwhile, were being courteously escorted through the streets with other pedestrians by the gardaí, who unwittingly helped them to make their way out of the town to safety. It turned out to be a case of mistaken identity: the gardaí had besieged the wrong bank.

CHAPTER 13

IN GOOD COMPANY

Life was not all bank raids, press conferences and interest rates, however. Through the job, I made many good friends. One larger-than-life character whose company was always a pleasure was Seamus Horgan of the *Cork Examiner*, a rotund figure whose beaming countenance was emphasised by a black beard that gave him a piratical appearance. He generally travelled with a cohort of colleagues from the paper acting as outriders. After five minutes in the company of these Cork men, I always found my own Cork accent beginning to seep back, and soon I would be speaking again in that sing-song idiom familiar to anyone who has lived in the shadow of Shandon's steeple.

Whenever I visited Cork, Seamus and his friends were always anxious to re-acquaint me with the delights of the city of my boyhood. Grand tours of its various watering holes would be arranged, and many enjoyable hours would be spent exchanging yarns with the legendary Katty Barry as she held court and entertained fellow-patrons in Dennehy's on the Coal Quay. (Katty once ran a famous late-night shebeen nearby which dispensed crubeens and well-watered whiskey.)

I recall leaving Dublin early one summer's morning to re-join the family in Schull, where our annual holidays had been interrupted for me by my having to attend an AIB-sponsored performance of the European Community Youth Orchestra in the RDS. On reaching Cork, I called in to the *Examiner* office and withdrew with Seamus, Noel Kelly and photographer, Des Barry, to Timmy O'Connor's on the Coal Quay for refreshments. It was a fine morning, sunlight shafting through the window as we exchanged news. Two elderly patrons ensconced in a corner were listening in as I made some reference to the concert of the previous evening. One of them immediately leaned in my direction with a look of avid interest.

'C'mere,' he asked, 'and what were de playin?'

I mentioned Berlioz's *Symphonie Fantastique*.

'Dere's a great waltz in de middle of dat!' he exclaimed, and proceeded to hum a bar or two. He fell into a reflective silence, then turned to me again. 'But c'mere,' he added, in classic Corkese, 'I'll tell 'oo summin' now – dere's no great symphonic tradition in Cork. Cork is *de voice*, boy!' He sat up with pride. 'Aren't we de only city in Ireland dat have an Opera House, an' choral festivals – amn't I right dere, Miah?' (turning to his companion). 'An' c'mere to me, where else would'oo find a Taoiseach dat can sing?'

My friendship with Seamus Horgan led to an unusual annual event: a coarse rugby match between a team from the bank (with guests) and a multi-talented *Examiner* fifteen, pitted against one another for what was known as the Bodhran Trophy. The object of these games, defined in one of their many unwritten rules, was to lose. They featured men who hurled themselves about with manic expressions suggestive of imminent coronary attacks, faces streaming and spreading paunches supported precariously by white, knobbly knees. The term 'prop forward' came into its own during these matches, as panting participants leaned on one another for long periods of physical support after random spasms of activity.

The final, glorious Bodhran outing took place on the Isle of Man. The decision to travel had something to do with the opening of an AIB office on the island, clinched by an agreement with the manager in Douglas, Gerry Nolan, that he would host the event. As part of the programme, Nolan was inspired to arrange a visit to the Okells brewery in Douglas on the morning of the match for the teams and their supporters, among them the well-known *Irish Times* news editor, Donal Foley, and his wife, Pat.

As a result of the hospitality at the brewery, the teams straggled on to the pitch later in the day in a decidedly unhealthy-looking state. The match itself was chiefly memorable for the fact that few of the players could remember much of it afterwards. By the cold light of Monday morning, however, some were showing signs of anxiety as they remembered their jobs and their bosses back home. One of the *Examiner's* photographers, Cyril Perrott (nicknamed 'the Flying Pencil') became particularly agitated. His glorious try of the previous day, when he had raced over the bank's line with the ball and, not fully understanding the rules, stood there while his team-mates begged him to ground it, was now forgotten.

To calm him, Seamus Horgan suggested to Cyril that he

should put in a phone-call to the paper's picture editor, Steve Coughlan, and explain the position candidly. A telephone was located, and we listened sympathetically to hear how Coughlan would take the news. The conversation – one side of it, at any rate – went as follows:

'Yes, Mr Coughlan. No, Mr. Coughlan. I know, Mr. Coughlan, I'm sorry. Look...Mr. Coughlan...I forgot to tell you the other day that I had a rugby match this weekend. Yes, Mr. Cough... No, no, I'm not injured – it's not that. The thing is, Mr. Coughlan, I won't actually be in the office until this afternoon. Where am I? – I'm in Douglas. What, Mr. Coughlan? Get the...? No, no, NO, Mr. Coughlan! Not *that* Doug...Mr. Coughlan? Mr. Coughlan...?'

He put the phone down slowly, looking a little pale. 'He's gone, Seamus,' he said glumly.

'What did he say?'

'He sounded very ratty. He told me to get on the bus and get into the office immediately.'

(For anyone not familiar with Cork, the city has a suburb called Douglas.)

~

Some of the friends I made through my job were truly extraordinary people, one or two of them defying all the laws of convention. One day in Merrion Row, I ran into Con Howard, whom I had first met in London when he was attached to the Irish embassy as counsellor in charge of media relations, a post created by the government in 1970 to help counteract the negative publicity being generated by the violence in Northern Ireland and the arms trial in Dublin.

Con was a legendary figure not only in Dublin and London, but also in Washington and in Boston, where he had begun his diplomatic career as consul general. I had barely set foot in London before I began to be asked, 'Have you met Con Howard yet?' On replying in the negative, I was invariably advised to make it my business to do so without delay.

I phoned the embassy, made an appointment and went along, not quite knowing what to expect. It turned out to be like encountering someone who has just experienced a beatific vision. Barely introduced, I was swept off to The King and Keys, where I was immediately swallowed up in his enthusiasm for his latest project, the St. Brendan Society. Before I had time to draw breath, I found that I had become a member of the steering committee. It was hard to be sure what I was getting into, but I did discover that this distinguished body had been inspired by Con's friendship with Tim Severin, who had recreated Saint Brendan's epic voyage to Newfoundland and had subsequently written the best-seller, *The Brendan Voyage*. Con was determined that the spirit of St. Brendan would be kept alive, and he outlined a dizzying array of ideas he had conceived for events and activities to be organised with the goal of furthering Irish-American social and cultural ties.

In the pub, I was introduced by Con to the essayist and powerful political editor of the *Daily Telegraph*, Peter T. E. Utley, a Tory whose virulent anti-Irish views did nothing to protect him from being co-opted immediately to the St. Brendan Society's steering committee. We were also joined by the Telegraph's gardening expert, Douglas Watson, a former Jesuit who wore a red rose in his buttonhole and began chanting Latin psalms at the sight of Con. 'Ah, Watson! You'll be coming too – you're on the committee!' declared Con, before breaking into his trademark anthem, the many-versed *Ballad of Tommy Daly* by Bryan MacMahon, delivered by Con in the sort of powerful tremolo voice that shatters windows in Marx Brothers films.

'*And from the broken northlands*
From the Burren bleak and bare
The dirge of Tommy Daly
Goes surging on through Clare.'

(I once heard Tip O'Neill, former US Speaker of Congress, describe Con's rendering of this ballad as doubtful singing, but definitely an art form.)

In my next recollection of that evening, it is after midnight and we have all adjourned to the upper floors of the Telegraph's offices where we have joined the paper's night workers in their canteen. Heaped plates of sausages and mash are being washed down by copious quantities of brown ale. Interestingly, the knives and forks are attached to the tables by chains. Con – who boasts an ample frontage which, like its owner, always seems to be about to burst free of restraint – is now standing on a table, from where, having won the hearts of his Cockney audience with the exploits of Tommy Daly, he is busy recruiting new members to the St. Brendan Society. He assures them that it has the support of the former British Prime Minster, Edward Heath, who has, it seems, been persuaded to chair one of its supporting committees (sailing section). By now, I am ready to believe him…and sure enough, some years later a member of the staff of the *Irish Times* who had met Ted Heath confirmed to me that the Tory politician had actually raised the matter with him.

If I digress with this story, it is because it contains some of the elements of the surreal which I soon discovered to be a defining characteristic of Con's many inventions, among them the Merriman and Shaw Summer Schools, the Byron Society and the Ireland-Australia Society. All his causes are promoted with the same terrifying missionary zeal. It is impossible to put a boundary around the imagination of Con Howard, scourge of bureaucrats and the mandarins of decorum in the Department of Foreign Affairs. It is also easy to underestimate the value of what he has achieved for Ireland through the wheels he has set in motion and friendships forged. It was largely due to Con that Ireland received an important bequest of paintings from the great Australian artist, Sir Sidney Nolan. In all the years I have known him, I have never heard him bad-mouth anyone, and it is suspected that much of the finance for his ventures comes from his own pocket.

But to return to our encounter in Merrion Row, both our London interludes now well behind us. As soon as Con spotted me, he prepared to hijack me with his latest project. This involved building a replica of the *Catalpa*, the four-masted whaling ship involved in the rescue of Fenians from the penal colony in Australia. My assistance was apparently needed. Con outlined the plot in his usual breathless shorthand.

'Epic voyage – re-enactment – financial backing – Tuesday, three o'clock – the *Asgard* – Alexandra Basin. Be there!

I gazed at his cherubic countenance: the ruddy cheeks, dishevelled white hair, demented bushy eyebrows shooting skywards in oblique lines. Con was always deadly serious about his schemes, even if his earnestness was regularly punctuated by manic bursts of laughter.

'Sounds terrific, Con,' I said (although some of the details had in fact passed me by).

'So you're with us, then?'

'Well…'

'Good man, good man.' He added: 'O'Reilly's coming! – he's putting up millions!' (Con also had a dream about making a film based on the *Catalpa* adventure, and he was attempting to persuade various potential backers – among them Tony O'Reilly

– to put up the money. Unfortunately, Con's enthusiasm would sometimes lead him to confuse the reality of what had been agreed with the desired outcome.)

The tide was out the following Tuesday as I walked down the quayside towards the *Asgard* and stared at what looked like an empty ship. Boarding, I heard a murmur of voices coming from the captain's quarters.

'You're late,' Con grumbled, as he introduced me to a dozen men of distinction from the marine world, who seemed pleased to meet me and shook my hand vigorously. Strewn across the table were architectural drawings of a sailing ship. The chief concern was whether the hull should be of steel or wood. After some debate, steel was decided upon, at a cost of some £7m. The eyes of the distinguished gathering turned to me.

'What do you think?' someone asked. I told him I thought it was a wonderful idea.

'Well, not so much that,' he said, 'but the money. Will the financial support be forthcoming, do you think? Will it be OK?'

The question took me by surprise. 'It's a bit outside my area,' I replied, 'but it's certainly worth making an approach to the bank.'

There was a brief silence.

'But,' someone finally asked, 'aren't you the chief executive?'

'Who, me?' I turned to Con, who seemed busy with a flurry of papers. 'O'Reilly,' he muttered. 'O'Reilly's the man.'

For all I know, the *Catalpa II* may be on the high seas even as I write.

CHAPTER 14

MAGIC!

One of the first steps AIB took when it was formed in 1970 was to establish a Marketing Department. It consisted initially of little more than a handful of people under Michael Carroll, and the public relations function fell loosely under its wing.

Carroll, a career banker, was one of the few genuine patrons of the arts I came across in banking, certainly in the Munster & Leinster. From modest beginnings, he built up a fine collection of Irish paintings. He was also an early member of *An Óige*, the Irish Youth Hostelling Organisation, and was among the first of us to venture forth on holidays to the continent. The fledgling Marketing Department that he headed up was a fairly independent unit, and I was happy to find myself there among some kindred spirits, including Angela Cotter, Brian McCarthy from Cork and Vincent O'Dea, who became one of my closest friends and remained so until his death in 1998. Something between Vincent and I seemed to set off a mutual sparking of the imagination that resulted in many a zany adventure over the following twenty-five years.

Vincent could always be counted upon to approach work – and life – from an oblique angle. Of medium height and build, he had a light complexion, pale lashes, thick eyebrows and fair, wavy hair. His movements were slow and measured, his expression grave, ponderous, sometimes even mournful. His smile, when it came, was slow with a hint of graciousness, half-hidden by the eternally upraised hand held close to his face, fingers bent inwards in loving embrace of the cigarettes which he smoked in life-threatening quantities with the unashamed pleasure of a child. Nothing of his true nature as a dreamer of impossible dreams and pursuer of improbable schemes was apparent in his demeanour as he frowned over the composition of a letter or hugged a bar counter from his perch on a stool, shoulders slightly hunched, legs crossed in languid pose.

He had a fine speaking voice, deep, sonorous and enriched by a warm Clare accent, but although he loved company and conversation, he could never have been described as talkative.

Indeed, if one listened carefully, much of his speech was actually thinking aloud: ruminating, speculating, deliberating. This permanent air of pondering arose from a conflict at the core of his being. On the one hand, Vincent was a deeply cautious man who needed the security of routine and familiar company and was inclined to be politely suspicious of people's motives; on the other, he was an innocent who harboured a passionate yearning for something bigger, grander, beyond himself. He was forever chasing 'magic', a word he used often.

The most constant of Vincent's dreams centred upon gaining a foothold in the world of entertainment and becoming rich in the process, and at several times it looked as if success might be within his grasp. He had genuine musical talent and was a fine pianist, less in the classical mould than in the style of the 1940s New York nightclub. He once wrote a song, *Christmas Candles*, which somehow found its way into the hands of Bing Crosby, who liked it so much that he decided to record it. It was released as a single and also appeared on a Crosby and Sinatra Christmas compilation album. Fame at last for Vincent! He dined out at length on this achievement, but his innocence of agents and record company executives left him with meagre reward for his efforts, and despite his attempts to repeat the coup, his name was soon forgotten by the music industry.

But Vincent was too canny to rely solely on his natural talents, and he kept a sharp eye out for other money-making opportunities. At one time, he imported secondhand tractors from England; at another, he acquired railway sleepers from disused lines, believing he could sell them for fencing to Tipperary farmers. He was convinced that there was a fortune to be made from antiques, which he suspected of lying undiscovered in old farmhouses around the country. He frequented auctions, often acquiring useless objects on the basis of wild hunches or even in error (he once came home with a large collection of outdated children's encyclopaedias which he had bid for by mistake in some confusion over lot numbers).

On the one occasion when Vincent's ship finally did come in, it turned out to be more of a paddle-boat than an ocean liner. He had an uncle, a parish priest in Flagmount, Co. Clare, who died leaving him a painting of an ugly-looking hound. The signature on the painting was illegible, but the frame bore a simple inscription: *Stubbs*. Vincent's hopes were high. If this were indeed the work of the eminent English painter, George Stubbs, it might, at last, make his fortune. Sotheby's agent in Dublin was summoned; he suggested that the painting be taken to London for further examination. Vincent departed immediately, his masterpiece in a green baize cloth under his arm.

In London, he linked up with a friend, Mike Burns of RTE, who was then based in the city. They decided they would try to have the painting assessed by the Tate Gallery. Vincent's account of this episode always conjured up for me a picture of an Irish Monsieur Hulot let loose in the Tate, causing accidental mayhem as he made his way from expert to expert, tripping over and almost destroying a valuable exhibit consisting of a pile of bricks on the ground.

As the Tate was unable to deliver a final verdict on the painting, the pair now made their way to Sotheby's, a short walk from the RTE office in Bruton Street. Here Vincent made himself comfortable in an antique chair while the Stubbs expert was summoned. He calmed his nerves by smoking, dropping the ash into a convenient bowl, in which he was also about to extinguish his cigarette when a horrified official intervened to protect what turned out to be a precious Ming urn.

Disappointingly, Sotheby's decided that the painting could not be attributed with certainty to Stubbs. They believed, however, that it could be the work of a pupil of the master, and suggested to Vincent that he enter it for auction in Sotheby's next sales. He agreed, and the following December the painting sold for some £6,000. It was not quite the fortune that Vincent had originally hoped to retire on, but it was a handy sum of money at the time.

Exhausted after all the excitement, Vincent now decided that he needed a holiday, and he took off for a week in the Canary Islands. He was new to foreign travel, however, and being a nocturnal creature by nature, he discovered that cavorting in the sea and acquiring a sun-tan were activities not to his taste. By the end of the week, he was glad to be heading home.

At the airport, a delay of six hours was announced. Vincent whiled away the time in the bar, drinking the cheap local brandy. As he sat there ruminating on life, an excited little man rushed in, waving his arms and urging Vincent to hurry as the plane was about to depart. Vincent finished up his drink, headed after the crowd and boarded. Shortly after take-off, he summoned a steward with a request to change some travellers' cheques. The steward disappeared and returned with a wad of notes, which Vincent studied in some surprise.

'I wonder could I have some sterling?' he enquired politely.

'Sterling?' The steward looked puzzled. 'Why you needa sterling?

'For when we get to Heathrow,' said Vincent reasonably.

The steward stared. 'Heathrow? But thisa plane isa nota going to London,' he said.

'So...where is it going then?' whispered Vincent, eyeing the unfamiliar banknotes with a sinking heart.

'To Eetaly!' the steward replied. 'Thisa plane isa going to Milano!'

Vincent's heart began to thump so rapidly that he decided he must be having a heart attack. The alarmed airline staff transferred him to a stretcher and emergency messages were radioed ahead to Milan. The sound of a wailing siren could be heard as the plane landed and he was carried off. Snow was falling, reminding him that he was dressed in light slacks and a short-sleeved shirt, and that his suitcase was probably by now in London.

In hospital, he was diagnosed with mild palpitations resulting from a touch of stress combined with Spanish brandy. It took the airline almost two days to sort the mess out, and after a prolonged incarceration in a hotel room (which Vincent was terrified to leave), he was finally flown to London and eventually reached home. It was an inglorious end to his brief career as an art dealer.

Vincent was above all an incurable romantic. He loved to listen to other people, particularly if he thought they came from the mystical land of Elsewhere, bearing tales of greener fields and gold just over the mountain. As a youngster he had run away from home to join the famous Anew MacMaster's travelling theatre company. He eventually submitted to the pressures of family and society and joined the bank, but at heart he remained an actor all his life, endlessly playing or dreaming himself into different roles: the musician, the poet, the serious banker, the film extra, the radio presenter, the upright citizen, the man about town, the impresario, the devout Christian, the insouciant bohemian.

In the early days of the new-style banking, the bank took to arranging various courses and lectures for staff. These were generally aimed at converting us to new ways of thinking and behaving that would improve customer relations and increase business. One of the first manifestations of this activity came in the form of a clean-cut young man in a shiny mohair suit from the Dale Carnegie Institute. (For anyone too young to remember, Dale Carnegie was an American whose world-famous book, *How To Win Friends and Influence People*, was the precursor of today's deluge of 'how to' books and management manuals.)

The Carnegie course was paid for by the bank: all we had to do was sign up and we could polish our social graces and learn to remember people's names. While many who attended such programmes did so only because they deemed it politically wise, Vincent had his own agenda. As we sat around reflecting on the course in advance, Vincent (who had a habit of speaking to and about himself in the third person) could be heard to muse, 'Yes…there could be possibilities in this for Vincent.'

By the end of his presentation, the dazzling young man from Dale Carnegie was looking pleased with himself, with the air of a man who knows he has done a good job. We were now invited to put questions to him on any point on which we were not clear. A few predictable queries were raised and swiftly dealt with. Then Vincent's arm slowly went up.

'Yes? Gentleman with the cigarette?'

'Tell me,' said Vincent, 'how did you get into this?'

'I beg your pardon? I didn't quite get the question.'

'Well, what shall I say,' Vincent smiled his most disarming smile. 'How do you get into this racket? I mean, how would one…how would I…shall we say…get into the business?'

Thrown off his guard, Dale Carnegie's disciple at first responded with good humour. Vincent (who was perfectly serious) gently persisted, and the session began to deteriorate, much to the delight of many of the audience. The young man became visibly agitated and started to display a definite dislike of the innocent saboteur. The exchange ended when he rather huffily threw in the towel and offered to give Vincent his money back. Vincent regarded him reproachfully. 'But I thought we were here to learn to make friends and influence people,' he said sadly, with an air of disillusionment.

Vincent and I concocted many schemes together over the years, some of them with a serious purpose related to the bank's marketing function, others largely for fun – although I think

Vincent always secretly hoped that even the most far-fetched of them might eventually strike gold. Ballygowan mineral water had been on the market for about a year when, in a moment of collective inspiration, we decided that there must surely be an opening for another spring water, from Vincent's native county, Clare, already famous for its healing spa at Lisdoonvarna and boasting a clean, unpolluted environment. In a state of heightened creativity, we hit upon the perfect name for the product. We even began to put together a catchy advertising jingle, to the tune of a familiar song:

All day we chased the Burren waste
Without the taste of water
Cool Clare Water.

Encouraged by this (although the product itself did not yet exist), we took ourselves off to the Companies Office and registered the company and the name, *Cool Clare Water*, appointing ourselves as directors. It happened that a friend of ours, a business journalist with RTE, was present at the moment of Cool Clare's conception. On the six-thirty business news the following day, he stunned its directors by announcing the company's set-up over the national airwaves! A week later he reported an expected 'take-over bid', and on yet another occasion he mentioned 'boardroom battles'.

Together, Vincent and I subsequently spent a long, hot summer's day scrabbling about the Burren in search of a source known locally as the Well of the Seven Sisters. Reputed for the quality of its water, it was said to achieve miraculous cures. Following the directions of an old man who told us that we would find the spring near a fairy tree, we located first the diminutive tree (by means of a rusty pendant attached to a branch, conveniently inscribed 'Fairy Tree'), and finally the well itself. Sadly, it was immediately obvious that the seven sisters would have to perform miracles if we were ever to fill more than a small cup from the meagre supply of water. Cool Clare Water has yet to commence trading.

Vincent's circle of acquaintances was huge. He was effectively the bank's promotions manager, and was involved in most of its sponsorship initiatives, including the GAA *Club of the Year* award. He was close to senior GAA officials, and always had a supply of tickets for all-Ireland football and hurling finals. On one occasion, the chairman of the bank, who had never been to Croke Park, sent him a message requesting four tickets for a final. The bank was entertaining the governors of some of Europe's Central Banks who were then visiting Dublin, and, having heard of its sporting and cultural significance, they had expressed an interest in attending the match. Vincent was reluctant to part with tickets generally reserved for friends, but eventually dispatched them to the chairman's office. Only at the last minute was it noticed that they were for Hill Sixteen rather than the Hogan or Cusack Stands. Replacements were demanded immediately. Vincent grudgingly obliged.

He also travelled around Ireland attending agricultural shows, local festivals and the like, where he would set up and man the AIB stand, sometimes accompanied by Angela Cotter and me. In this way we visited many parts of the country together, staying in small hotels and socialising dutifully with the local KBIs.

An annual event at which Vincent represented the bank in this way was the Royal Agricultural Show at Stonely in England. On one occasion there he learned that Her Majesty, the Queen Mother, would be in attendance, and following royal custom, she was expected to walk around and view some of the stands. Unknown to the security staff and Her Royal Self, Vincent rearranged her route. He somehow managed to move the ropes guiding her footsteps so that she would be led directly across the AIB stand, where he waited in ambush with a hired photographer, hidden behind a large pot-plant.

Everything went according to plan. Accompanied by a retinue of men in dark suits, the Queen Mother moved slowly along, smiling, waving to the applauding crowd and occasionally stopping to talk to someone, until she suddenly found herself at the AIB stand. Ready for action, Vincent shot forward, grasped her hand firmly, welcomed her on behalf of the bank and presented her with an AIB plastic moneybox. As she thanked him warmly, with a gracious, 'How sweet of you! It's just what one of my grandchildren needs,' the photographer jumped out from behind the foliage and aimed his Hasselblad. Just as quickly, the men in dark suits sprang into action, seizing the moneybox and the camera for inspection, ordering the photographer to join the press corps on the other side of the group, and glaring threateningly at Vincent. Completely unabashed, he proceeded to engage the Queen Mother in a conversation that glossed quickly over the bank's activities in Britain to move on to more important topics, such as his acquaintance (almost) with the great Bing Crosby, and his song, *Christmas Candles*.

The photograph, which Vincent had hoped would have worldwide release, made its appearance in print some weeks later. It was not in *The Times*, the *Telegraph* or the *Guardian*, nor in the *Irish Times* or *Irish Press*. It was on the front page of *An Phoblacht*, and the caption, presumably humorous, referred to 'a pair of old relics'.

When Vincent retired from the bank, he wasted little time before pursuing further one of his many long-held dreams: to become a radio broadcaster. With the help of a friend, Camin Jones of *Clare FM*, this time the dream finally came true, and Vincent's mellow voice soothed and entertained listeners in Clare and the surrounding counties every Sunday morning with an hour-long programme of music and stories, *Memories*. Much of the material for the programme was assembled late at night in the Arts Club in Upper Fitzwilliam Street or the snug of Doheny & Nesbitt's, and the music often came from old records borrowed from friends.

The programme lasted for several years, until indifferent health and the weekly journey to Ennis began to take its toll. Of all the roles that Vincent played, I think it was the one that gave him the most satisfaction, for it set his imagination loose to wander freely.

Vincent's departure from this life seemed somewhat out of keeping with his character. We probably expected something more flamboyant. Yet perhaps it was the real Vincent who played out his last act, slipping quietly away in his sleep. After the funeral, a few of his friends who had shared in his many adventures retired to a pub within earshot of where he had been laid to rest. Fulfilling a promise made partly in jest years before, I had brought along an elderly gramophone, and as we reminisced and exchanged stories of Vincent, I placed it on the bar counter and carefully dropped a record on the turntable. After a scratchy start, the unmistakable voice of Bing Crosby filled the air above our bowed heads:

Light a penny candle
On a Christmas tree.

We raised a glass to the composer.

CHAPTER 15

GIANTS

One day in the Marketing Department, another of the parachutists I mentioned earlier landed among us. He was a harbinger of a world yet to come. As head of marketing and technology, J. Finbarr Donovan wasted little time in acquainting himself with his foot-soldiers. His first step was to convene a meeting at which he briskly sketched the future and began assigning roles. His attentive platoon of greenhorns sensed they were about to board the big dipper and were already fastening their seat-belts when a phone call interrupted. Donovan took the call, grabbed his coat and disappeared out the door, indicating that the discussion would resume at another time. Hours later we discovered that he was now somewhere over the Atlantic headed in the direction of Canada. It was a far cry from the days when 'travel' meant an outing to a sub-office in Maynooth or a transfer to Kildysart, and we knew that exciting times lay ahead.

We soon discovered that Finbarr Donovan was more than just another high-powered executive. His vast knowledge of technology – still rare at the time – was one of the main reasons for his appointment, but it quickly became apparent that he was also a kind of modern Renaissance man. His grasp of integrated circuits, modems, applied science and the jargon of marketing combined effortlessly with a passion for history, art, philosophy, medieval architecture and the antiquities of Greece, Rome and Egypt. He took great pleasure in dismantling outmoded conventions and practices, and he brought a breath of fresh air to pen-and-ink banking.

One of Finbarr's more creative conscripts in the Marketing Department was Brian McCarthy. Son of Denis McCarthy, whom I have already mentioned as the bank's first agricultural relations officer, Brian was a big man in every sense. I once heard him described as a cross between two giants: the journalist and writer, Con Houlihan, and Moss Keane, the international rugby player. Brian was warm and generous, with an easy-going nature that belied a creative mind and a keen organisational ability that could bring complex concepts to reality. We became good friends, and continue so today.

In the bank, Brian McCarthy was fairly orthodox in most respects, but he also had a refreshingly independent turn of mind and was not beyond ruffling a few feathers if necessary. Supported by Finbarr Donovan, who actively encouraged innovation in those who worked under him, he produced a steady stream of new ideas, some of which may have raised eyebrows in the higher echelons of banking. The good sense that had initially identified his ability and moved him from the Foreign Department to Marketing unfortunately did not prevail. In August 1974, he was suddenly transferred to Killorglin, Co. Kerry, as assistant manager of the branch. There, although he worked successfully for years alongside the well-respected manager, John O'Connell (brother of the great Kerry footballer, Mick O'Connell), he was advised by the regional office in Tralee that he was unlikely ever to be promoted to the position of manager.

Personnel departments (somewhat chillingly referred to today as 'human resources') are susceptible to basing opinions on thumbnail sketches that can elevate people's reputations or damn them forever. I have little doubt that Brian McCarthy fell foul of this kind of stupidity. He may simply not have conformed to some accepted notion of 'management material', because someone somewhere lacked the imagination to recognise his talents.

For the bank, it turned out to be a lamentable mistake. During the 1966 strike, Brian had taken to boarding tourist coaches in Killarney and offering to change foreign currencies at official Central Bank rates. With the banks closed at the height of the tourist season, he had no shortage of customers. He carefully filed the success of that venture away for future reference, realising that the limited opening hours and range of services offered by Irish banks would one day create an opening for a competitor.

The Central Bank had been concerned about the country's bureau de change system for years. Outside of the banks, foreign exchange transactions were being conducted on an *ad hoc* basis in a variety of outlets, and there was little control over the rates of exchange being offered. Meanwhile, the banks' short opening hours (from ten in the morning until three in the afternoon, with an hour's closure for lunch) fell well short of public need.

Brian McCarthy now decided that it was time to put into action a plan that had been germinating in his mind since the strike. He put before the Central Bank a detailed proposal which convinced them that he had the expertise to set up and efficiently run an authorised bureau de change company in Ireland. He obtained the necessary approval, and with the support of a friend, Ed Crowley, resigned from his secure, pensionable job in the bank and opened for business. His company, *The Foreign Exchange Company of Ireland*, began trading in January 1985 in a small room over Jemma's Hairdressing Salon in Killorglin. Later, he purchased the old railway station on the edge of the town and began the expansion of his bureau de change offices throughout the country under the name of FEXCO.

It was a bold move, but it was just the beginning. Further expansion came with a system for reimbursing the VAT paid by non-EU visitors on purchases made during their stay in Ireland. To handle the rapid development of his company, Brian needed expertise in advanced computer technology. He turned – where else? – to his former mentor and colleague, Finbarr Donovan, whose technological skills had given AIB a significant lead in that area in Ireland. With Donovan's assistance, the most advanced system available was installed in the converted railway station in Killorglin.

Next, Brian decided to try to capture a segment of the UK market for VAT reimbursements, having noted that no UK company was capitalising fully on the opportunities offered by the European legislation. It happened that a young Englishwoman, Mary Loftus, was entertaining customers with her piano playing at Nick's restaurant in Killorglin during the summer. Nick's had become FEXCO's executive dining centre, and Brian (no mean pianist himself) invited her to consider spearheading a drive by FEXCO on the London market. She proved herself an energetic and tenacious saleswoman, who soon persuaded some of London's major department stores to entrust the worldwide reimbursement of their customers' VAT to the young Kerry company.

This success was followed by FEXCO taking over the processing of the Prize Bonds (previously handled by the Bank of Ireland), a development celebrated in style in Killorglin when the citizens of Puck turned out in the dead of night to cheer a convoy of trucks carrying millions of Prize Bonds to FEXCO's headquarters, protected by an Army escort.

A period of international expansion followed in both Europe and the US. FEXCO also became agent in Ireland, Britain and much of continental Europe for Western Union, the world's oldest electronic money transfer business.

In short, FEXCO has been a phenomenal success, winning many awards along the way. Throughout the years, Brian's banking friends in Dublin have followed his company's dramatic rise, taking much pride in the achievements of one who was once virtually written off by the bank. He remains unchanged, a man from whose company one emerges feeling enriched, as passionate about classical music and sport as about his business, and probably happiest today out in a boat somewhere around the Skelligs.

~

The loss of Brian McCarthy was a blow to his colleagues in the Marketing Department, but life went on, and for me, one of the better aspects of my job was the access it gave me to a wide variety of interesting people.

As already discussed in a previous chapter, the formation of the two main banking groups in the early 1970s saw the banks begin to involve themselves in sponsorships, particularly in sport and in the arts. It was good timing for the arts especially, as the country was slowly emerging from decades of rigid censorship and other, less formal constraints. There was a sense of growing freedom in the air. Small Irish publishers were beginning to spring up. Local theatrical societies were flourishing, new galleries were opening, music – particularly traditional music – was thriving, and the need for a national concert hall was beginning to be discussed. Flexing their financial muscles, the banks took note. As far back as fifteenth-century Florence, there had always been a tradition of patronage of the arts by financial institutions in Europe, and happily, there were some in AIB who genuinely believed the bank could play a useful role in this respect beyond pure self-interest.

Together with Dermot Egan, head of human resources, I remember paying a visit to the studio (known as *The Skullery*) of the sculptor, Seamus Murphy, in Blackpool, Cork, where we purchased three pieces on behalf of the bank. The bronze head of his father and *The Tailor of Gougane Barra*, along with a delicate piece entitled *Prayer*, are probably among his finest work. They were among the first acquisitions in what went on to become a substantial collection of Irish art assembled by the bank. Thereafter, the pace of its patronage quickened, and with the completion of its new headquarters in Ballsbridge (known as *Bankcentre*), a specific arts committee was established. Dr. Frances Ruane was engaged as consultant advisor and buyer to invest in quality paintings and sculpture, with an emphasis on contemporary Irish art of the twentieth century.

Sponsorship of the arts in a wider sense now began to take off. A social affairs committee had been formed under the chairman of the bank, Niall Crowley, and from its initial agenda of contributing to charity, it decided to broaden its scope. With the backing of the bank's deputy chairman, Professor Patrick Lynch, and group chief executive, Joe McGlinn, AIB launched an annual award for literature. Chosen to adjudicate was the Irish Academy of Letters, founded by George Bernard Shaw and W. B. Yeats, whose membership included most of the country's distinguished novelists, poets and playwrights.

The presentation of the AIB Literary Awards became for a time one of the highlights of the literary year, and preparation for the event brought me into contact with many interesting people connected with the Academy, both members and non-members. I gradually got to know and enjoy the company of the likes of Benedict Kiely, Sean MacReamoin, Mary Lavin and Sean White. Journalists of a literary bent were also sometimes involved, among them Donal Foley of the *Irish Times*, John Ryan (an Academy member), Paddy Downey, Con Houlihan, Mike Burns and Raymond Smith.

The presentation ceremony usually took place after a 'literary lunch' or dinner at an appropriate venue, sometimes in one of the bank's more architecturally interesting buildings. They were marvellous occasions, enlivened by a sparkling flow of conversation, story-telling and humour. It was a pleasure to find oneself in the company of people whose talent and intellectual abilities were matched by a capacity for enjoying life, and who took themselves less than seriously.

The awards themselves varied: one might honour a particular work; another a lifetime's achievement. Among the special awards I particularly remember was one presented to Mary Lavin in recognition of her contribution to Irish literature. It was decided that the presentation should take place in Sligo to coincide with the handing over of an AIB branch office to the Yeats Society for use as a permanent home and exhibition centre. To celebrate the occasion in style, a special train was commissioned to convey the party to Sligo with the help of Sean White, then head of public affairs in CIE. A miscellany of poets, writers and camp-followers left Dublin in a sumptuously appointed carriage lit by flickering candles. Amid sparkling cutlery and polished glass, they were wined and dined courtesy of AIB as they clickety-clanked their way across the country.

The following day, the presentation completed, we started to think about making our way back to Dublin. Looking after Irish writers is no small matter, however, especially when they have consumed generous quantities of vintage wine and port. They are of an independent turn of mind, and supervising mice at a crossroads would have been easier than herding the party successfully towards the railway station and aboard the Dublin train.

There was worse to come. With everyone finally seated, the truth began to dawn. The returning locomotive was not in the same league as the refined version that had made the outward journey. It was, in fact, the regular Sligo-Dublin train, but we, the organisers, had vaguely assumed that it would be adequate and would provide the basic facilities, such as a bar. Not so. The ancient vehicle staggered to a halt at every station and crossing along the way, sometimes coming to a standstill in the middle of a boggy field for no apparent reason. Worse still was that there was nothing in the way of refreshments: no food of any kind, no bar, not as much as a cup of tea to calm the rising anxieties of the literary party – not that tea was uppermost on their minds.

Long before the creaking train was halfway to Dublin, something close to despair had set in. Hopes rose briefly in Longford when it pulled in alongside a superior train facing in the opposite direction and a seriously-dehydrated Ben Kiely, president of the Irish Academy of Letters, succeeded in attracting the attention of a barman on the other train, at arm's length from an open window. Just as a transaction involving a bottle of whiskey was about to be completed, the Dublin train slowly moved off. Irish writers' capacity to use language with colour and passion was demonstrated to the full as they watched the barman fade into the distance. Eventually Dublin was reached, and an evening in the bar of the Shelbourne Hotel was needed to soothe the weary travellers. The lesson in public relations for the bank was clear: if you send a party out in style, make sure you can bring them home in similar manner.

~

Corporate sponsorships tend to favour only the more popular and established manifestations of the arts, and money is rarely bestowed on new or experimental work. The New York office of AIB once agreed to sponsor the opening night of *The Great Hunger*, the contemporary Irish play by Tom MacIntyre which was to be staged on Broadway by the Abbey Theatre. The Abbey would have been seen by the bank as 'kosher' – a pearl in the country's cultural heritage. It is possible that no one in the bank had ever seen or read the play, or even enquired about the plot. The fact that it was being presented by the Abbey was enough: the sponsorship would boost the image of the bank.

A *Who's Who* of New York was invited to the opening night: business moguls heads of leading financial institutions, society queens, even the cardinal archbishop of New York. The chairman of AIB, Niall Crowley, was whisked across the Atlantic for the occasion.

Ten minutes into the production, many of the audience had already begun to squirm in their seats. This was strong stuff, far from the Kathleen Mavourneens and Celtic mists-that-do-be-on-the-bog that they were probably expecting. Some, perhaps in a state of shock, or simply deciding to forego the play in favour of the free bar, failed to re-appear after the first act. The rumour whispered around subsequently was that someone in AIB had mistaken MacIntyre's play for Cecil Woodham Smith's book of the same name about the Famine. Therein lay perhaps a *second* lesson in arts sponsorship for the bank: first read the book!

CHAPTER 16

LANDMINES

Much as I would have enjoyed confining my role in the bank to activities such as the literary awards, I was inevitably called upon at times to acquaint myself more intimately with the world of finance, and even on occasion to demonstrate an appreciation of its intricacies. This sometimes meant skating on precariously thin ice.

One autumn morning as I was enjoying a leisurely cup of coffee with Vincent O'Dea and Angela Cotter, I was summoned to present myself immediately before Paddy O'Keeffe, general manager (banking). Known to some as the Great White Chief, O'Keeffe had a presence that inspired awe, if not terror. Even his appearance – pale complexion, steely blue eyes and angular features – suggested a formidable character. Paddy O'Keeffe was not given to small talk or backslapping bonhomie. His tendency was to cut to the point, and when presented with news not to his taste, he was said to be capable of swallowing a dozen bankers before lunch.

Making my way to his office, I straightened my tie and knocked on the door.

'Come in!'

I stepped into the room and glanced around. It was a large and suitably impressive office. The Great White Chief, surrounded by a cluster of serious-faced executives, presided over it with an air of unmistakable authority from behind a vast leather-topped desk which seemed a long way from the door.

'Ah, it's you,' he said, in brisk tones. 'I want your advice. Sit down.' He indicated a chair. 'Right,' he began, 'I'll give you an outline of the problem.'

He proceeded to summarise the facts behind a rather sticky situation that had developed, involving an important corporate client and a substantial loan which O'Keeffe feared might have vanished into the ground. The incident was almost sure to have unpleasant repercussions for the bank should the media start probing the story. It was a complicated affair, and as he strode briskly through the main points, I struggled to grasp its nuances. The exposé ended rather abruptly.

‘Well,’ he demanded, ‘what action do you think we should take?’

I coughed and shifted my position slightly. ‘What action do I think we should take?’ I echoed, playing for time and giving my mind a chance to do its usual trick and slip into automatic gear. It did not fail me. ‘Well,’ I began jauntily, ‘there are two ways of looking at this. On the one hand…’

‘Stop!’ O’Keeffe interrupted, his eyes burning holes in mine. ‘I didn’t ask you for a *choice!* I need *precise* advice – not a list of alternatives.’

Precision had never been one of my strong points, but desperate situations call for desperate measures, and the look on his face had a wonderfully concentrating effect on my mind.

‘Mr. O’Keeffe,’ I said, assuming my gravest expression, ‘my advice would be to give the financial editors the full story before someone else informs them and approaches it from another angle – one that might not be good for the bank. Give them the bank’s side of the story – now.’

The room held its breath. O’Keeffe bowed his head in thought for a moment. He then turned to Ned O’Callaghan, a trusted senior executive.

‘Ned,’ he said. ‘I want you to imagine you’re Richard Keatinge, the financial editor of the *Irish Times*. And you,’ turning to me, ‘you go outside, come in casually, imagine you’re walking into Keatinge’s office and give Ned the story. The rest of you may leave,’ he added, glancing around at the remaining members of the cast.

This was a turn of events I hadn’t envisaged. The details of the situation so recently outlined were already growing fuzzy in my brain. I exited, murmured a quick prayer and knocked before re-entering on cue. Ned O’Callaghan, leaning comfortably back in his chair, was looking amused. Feeling awkward and not quite knowing what was expected, I decided to give it my all. I eased my backside onto O’Keeffe’s desk with theatrical nonchalance, one leg swinging casually. O’Callaghan’s eyes widened slightly. He threw an anxious glance in O’Keefe’s direction. I was briefly tempted to pull out my pipe, but thought better of it.

‘Good morning, Richard – how are you?’ I began, enunciating exaggeratedly.

Ned threw himself into the part: ‘Well, hello, Bob! What brings you to this neck of the woods?’

'Ah, sure I happened to be passing and I thought I'd drop in and say hello.'

For some reason, we were both speaking rather loudly. The preliminaries over, a pause followed. It was Ned's move. 'What's all this I hear about the collapse of X?' he asked, tilting his head to one side with the air of an intelligent canary.

'Ah, nothing to get excited about. I suppose you've heard they're going into liquidation.'

A strangled cry came from across the desk. I had walked on a landmine.

'It's a RECEIVERSHIP!' O'Keeffe roared. 'A receivership! We're putting in a receiver – not a liquidator.' He put his head between his hands. 'Start again! Go outside and come in again.'

Exit the man from AIB, stage left.

Once again, I knocked on the door. My throat had gone dry and my knees were feeling weak. I entered.

'Good-morning-Richard. How-are-you?' Somehow the spontaneity had gone out of it.

'Well-hello-Bob.What-brings-you-to-this-neck-of-the-woods?' (Ned was clearly enjoying himself, and there was a twinkle of mischief in his eye that I didn't like.) He continued: 'What's all this I hear about a *receiver* being appointed to X?'

I began promisingly but my tongue took off on a tack of its own, and before long I was interrupted by another explosion from O'Keeffe.

'What are you saying?' he howled. 'He asked you one question and you're answering two! Why are you answering a question you weren't asked at all? Go out and start again.'

Weary, I exited. I briefly considered faking a cardiac arrest or an epileptic fit.

Eventually I was released and despatched on my mission to meet the financial editors of the various newspapers. I headed into town to perform before a live audience. I decided it would be a good idea to call first on Joe MacAuley, who had become financial editor of the *Irish Press* after taking early retirement from the Bank of Ireland. The rehearsals had given me a fearful thirst, and I was grateful when Joe suggested we retire to Mulligan's, where we discussed a wide range of topics of mutual interest. He touched at some stage on the thorny issue of X. My practised explanation seemed to satisfy him.

As I headed for the *Irish Times*, it occurred to me that he had not seemed hugely interested. This was encouraging, and sure enough, it turned out to be the case with Richard Keatinge too. I then crossed O'Connell Bridge and made my way to Middle Abbey Street to Colm Rapple of the *Irish Independent*, returning via the Ha'penny Bridge to call on Tony Ring, Dublin editor of the *Cork Examiner*. Once again, this time in the Temple Bar around the corner, the conversation ranged over many matters. Once again, only slight interest was shown in the real purpose of my visit.

It had been a long day, but the conviviality had revived me. I returned to Pembroke Road around seven in the evening, hoping that everyone would have gone home. Alas, no – the lights in Paddy O'Keeffe's window were still glowing. I made my way to his office and found O'Keeffe, O'Callaghan and the original team still in session, somewhat nervously awaiting my return.

'Well?' Anxious eyes surveyed me.

'No problem,' I assured them. 'It's a non-runner.'

Gasps. 'But why?'

'Too complex. Not enough hard facts. Not enough information.'

'Are you sure?' O'Keeffe fixed me intently with his eye.

'Certain.'

'You're absolutely certain?'

'I'm certain.'

Like magic, the atmosphere relaxed. Ned O'Callaghan and the others were sent home. A bottle of Glenfiddich single malt whiskey appeared. Paddy O'Keeffe put an arm around my shoulder. 'You know,' he said, 'Your father and I were great friends in Cork.'

~

Probably the best known and certainly the longest internal dispute in the bank's history involved a man for whom I have great regard, Niall Murphy. Like his older brother, John (with whom, the reader may recall, I once had the pleasure of dining *gratis* on *Sole Bonne Femme*), Niall was at one time captain of Clontarf Rugby Club, taking the team to a Leinster Senior Cup Final and imbuing them with his own kamikaze-like courage and determination to win.

In the late 1960s, Niall was among the first of the banking fraternity to discover that because of their high silver content,

Irish silver coins minted pre-1943 and British coins pre-1922 were worth more than their face value. As word spread, tellers in all the banks began to collect them. They were easy to spot in a pile of loose change because of their distinctive size and colouring. Before long, shopkeepers, parish priests, rent collectors, owners of amusement arcades and guardians of stiles at football matches were all eagerly on the trail of the silver bullion. The Central Bank, then a rather toothless tiger, issued mild requests for the banks' cooperation in retrieving the silver, but with little success. Niall Murphy meanwhile honed his skills in the matter and became acquainted with dealers in coins. In later years, after this mini-Klondyke had led to a heightened interest in coin collecting, he became an expert numismatist and a dealer in coins, commemorative medals and general memorabilia.

Niall's dispute with the bank arose in Rush, Co. Dublin, when he was assistant manager of the branch. It began simply enough. With the manager's approval, certain customers were being allowed access to the bank after official closing time. The IBOA representative in the branch objected to this after-hours business and locked the door of the bank, signalling a dispute. For whatever reason, the union head office did not back him, but Murphy did, and together they continued the dispute.

AIB senior executives motored hurriedly to Rush to try and settle the problem, but were refused entry. The bank took disciplinary action. Unwilling to give ground, the pair continued their protest, were suspended and decided to battle it out, picketing the gates of Bankcentre and erecting placards on the railings. For Niall Murphy in particular this was a matter of honour, and the only solution he would accept was one that satisfied his sense of justice and his self-esteem. The bank was not used to such action and refused to give in.

After lengthy negotiations and Labour Court appearances, Murphy's co-rebel eventually agreed to a settlement, which Niall rejected outright. The situation had reached an impasse. The whole affair began to look more like a personal battle of wits between him and certain members of AIB's executive rather than simple adherence to the bank's principles and procedures. Many of those in the bank who took a hard line in the matter believed that Murphy would soon tire and the wretched affair would fade quietly away.

Twenty years and four successive AIB chairmen later, the

conflict continues unresolved, despite the best efforts of various well-intentioned people. In the role of the boy David, Niall Murphy descends each year on the bank's AGM with his small band of supporters, bent on disruption (as the holder of bank shares, he is entitled to have his say). He launches slingshots in the form of awkward questions and filibustering, while exasperated shareholders – mostly bank pensioners out for the day – shout 'sit down' and 'tut-tut'. It is hard to believe that an institution which regularly deals with complex issues in which millions of pounds are at stake cannot resolve a problem involving one of its own former assistant managers, a man whose father and brother were respected managers in the same institution.

The saga of Niall Murphy versus the bank does, however, offer an interesting example of a company shareholder exercising his right to challenge the board in a way probably not anticipated by the founding fathers of public companies. Semi-state bodies heading for privatisation, take note!

~

It was around this time that I had the dubious pleasure of first hearing myself on national radio. I was the guest of Peter Murphy of *Macra na Feirme* fame on his popular weekly programme. This was always pre-recorded, the format being a brief interview followed by a piece of music of the guest's choice.

'Tell me now, Mr. Bob (*sic*),' Murphy concluded the session, 'would you care to select a favourite record?'

My mind went back to an evening with some friends in Brian McCarthy's apartment some weeks previously. A wonderful recording of Beethoven's Ninth Symphony was playing in the background, and Brian had suddenly silenced us: 'Listen to this magnificent adagio.'

I seized the opportunity to demonstrate my good taste in music to the nation. 'Thank you, Peter. Could I have the adagio from Beethoven's Ninth?'

'Yes, indeed, Mr. Bob – a fine choice. And now, this is Peter Murphy saying goodbye to our listeners and signing off on behalf of Monica Carr and myself with a special request for our guest of today, Bob Ryan of AIB. Here is the adagio from Beethoven's Ninth Symphony.'

The programme was scheduled to go out the following Saturday, and family and friends had been alerted. The short interview (something to do with travelling banks) seemed to go quite well. Peter Murphy brought it to a close, and I sat back in my chair feeling rather pleased as I prepared to listen to Beethoven and enhance my image as a man of culture. I stared at the radio in disbelief as the host ended the programme cheerily: 'And this is Peter Murphy…signing off…with a special request for our guest of today, Bob Ryan of AIB. Here is Big Tom and the Mainliners, with *The Four Roads to Glenamaddy!*' He knew his audience all too well.

CHAPTER 17

IN THE HEADLINES

The completion of *Bankcentre* in 1979 marked a radical shift in AIB's corporate profile and positioning in the marketplace. Previously, the various divisions of Head Office were scattered over at least half a dozen buildings around Dublin, reinforcing the fragmented image suggested by the plural in *Allied Irish Banks*. The acquisition of a thirteen-and-a-half acre site adjoining the railway line in fashionable Ballsbridge, purchased from the RDS in March 1973 at a cost of £4.3m, was a significant step in the consolidation of the old three-in-one bank into the new, single entity, AIB.

The guiding hand behind the development of the bank's new headquarters was that of Jim Fitzpatrick, then chief executive. In the face of internal pressure to fill the ample space exclusively with offices, Fitzpatrick insisted on a low-rise, campus-style complex where today, attractive landscaping and the imaginative use of plants soften and enhance the buildings. Internally, the design was largely open-plan. Brightly coloured screens were rumoured to have been chosen for their supposed capacity to help stimulate ambitions, fire imaginations and increase levels of application to the job – a notion roundly dismissed by the more cynical elements of the staff, not impressed by such psycho-babble.

The project was brought to reality through the vision of the architect, Andy Devane, and the complex was formally opened by the Taoiseach, Charles Haughey, on 19 February 1980, providing AIB for the first time with a national and international focus for its growing range of activities.

~

An army marches on its stomach, they say, and to those of us who found ourselves plucked from various offices around the city and thrown together in the vast new complex that was Bankcentre, one of its great successes lay in its catering department. I do not mean this flippantly: corporate entertainment was taking on a new meaning at this time, and a top team in the kitchen was important beyond the task of merely keeping the workers happy.

The appointment of Ollie MacMahon as head of catering was a stroke of genius. Ollie introduced award-winning chefs of international calibre, capable of generating banquets of exquisite style and impressing even the most fastidious gourmets. He also brought with him a number of the great professional head waiters who had once graced the grand old hotels of Dublin, like the Russell and the Royal Hibernian. Among them were Michael Nolan, Gerry Duff and Sean Tierney. 'What's your pleasure, sah?' Gerry Duff, a former army man, would enquire, anticipating visitors' every need and giving them a sense of their own importance. Apart from their professional skills, the waiters' distinctive personalities and charm added colour to the otherwise grey business of banking.

The feats of Ollie and his staff brought a new dimension to the art of winning friends and influencing people. In well-appointed private dining rooms at elegantly laid tables, they catered for everyone from government ministers, foreign financiers and captains of industry to dairy and tillage farmers, horse breeders, members of local community associations, hurlers from pitch and ditch, and kickers of round and oval balls.

On one memorable occasion they even found themselves playing host to the abbots (and a lone abbess) from the country's Cistercian monasteries, there at the invitation of the head of marketing and technology, J. Finbarr Donovan, whose vision and interests, as I have already mentioned, went far beyond what was usual in the bank. The incongruity of robed monks canting *none* in austere plainchant before a good lunch in the high temple of banking provoked another guest at that meal, film producer and former RTE executive, Muiris MacConghail, to remark that he regretted not having a camera crew to hand.

At Christmas, the season of goodwill really got under way with a lunch in Bankcentre for the RTE News Division. It was an event that was greatly looked forward to, an annual get-together with some of the brightest minds in that organisation, including the head of news, Wesley Boyd; news editor, Peadar Keogh, with his deputy, Eddie Liston; newsreaders, Charles Mitchell, Anne Doyle and Eileen Dunne; and the likes of Sean Duignan, Andrew Sheppard, Mike Burns, Brendan Keenan, Kevin Healy, Ella

Shanahan and various other newshounds known to be good raconteurs and good company. The windows looking out on John Behan's majestic sculpture, *Megalith*, would become steamed up as hod toddies worked their magic on the gathering and the strains of song mingled in the corridors with lingering aromas from the kitchen. Later, Gerry Duff and Sean Tierney would solicitously see to it that the walking wounded were guided home safely, while hardier souls headed in the direction of the nearby Horse Show House.

An episode that always comes to mind when I remember this period began with a lunch in Bankcentre and ended with Ronald Reagan's scriptwriter, Dana Rowenbacker, facing a hostile crowd in Lahinch, Co. Clare.

Rowenbacker and one of Reagan's chief legal advisors were visiting Ireland from the White House. They had been enrolled by Con Howard as members of the Washington chapter of the St. Brendan Society, and invited by him to attend the annual Merriman Summer School in Lahinch, Co. Clare, where the unsuspecting Rowenbacker was to address an equally unsuspecting Merriman gathering with a paper on aspects of President Reagan's foreign policy.

It was the Americans' first time in Ireland, and to steady them for their mission, a lunch had been arranged in Bankcentre. After an excellent meal together, we boarded the luxury coach that was to bear the party in style to Co. Clare. Just as it was about to depart, Gerry Duff approached the driver and discreetly entrusted him with a napkin, containing, as he delicately explained, a pair of false teeth found on a table amid the remnants of the Beef Wellington. No one seemed anxious to claim ownership, but Con Howard put them carefully in his pocket, ostensibly for safe-keeping.

We eventually arrived in Lahinch and assembled in the town's recreation centre on the seafront, where President Hilary addressed a welcome to the 'Merrimen' and women. Throughout his speech, strange cries in a strong Clare accent came from the larger room next door: 'All the yellows, forty-five! Ten for blue, good for you! Green: clickety-click, sixty-six! Sixteen: black at the back! And we have a check! Hold it now!' I saw the look of bewilderment on Dana Rowenbacker's face and leaned towards him: 'Bingo,' I whispered. He nodded, but continued to look perplexed.

Between one thing and another, it was well after midnight by the time the US President's scriptwriter was invited to deliver his paper to a now somewhat tired group of Merriman devotees, corralled in an upper room of the Claremont Hotel by Con Howard (who had now restored the unclaimed teeth to their proper place) and other members of the committee. They were decidedly not in the mood for the thoughts of Ronald Reagan, and as Rowenbacker's talk proceeded, they became testy and started to heckle, putting the man from the White House under extreme pressure. With such penetrating questions as, 'Who dropped the first atomic bomb?' being hurled at him, and the event looking in danger of complete disintegration, Con Howard, who had appointed me as chairman, suddenly reappeared by my side.

'Make an announcement,' he whispered urgently. 'Tell them the bar has re-opened down below.'

In the rush that followed, Dana Rowenbacker was swept downstairs by the tide of rejuvenated Merrimen, who forgot their hostility and dug into their pockets to stand the decent man from the White House a pint of stout. After a few sips of Guinness, Rowenbacker was called on for a song. He immediately pulled a small lyre-shaped instrument, a Jew's-harp, from his pocket, put it between his teeth and began merrily twanging *Dixie*. I would love to have heard the man's own version of his first day in Ireland.

~

As the range of services provided by Irish banks continued to expand, their marketing and public relations offices grew busier. The banks had begun to rationalise the branch system around the country, sometimes closing branches and sub-offices, a move that caused considerable local resentment. (This issue is still very much alive today.) They moved into the area of house loans, traditionally the preserve of the building societies, and introduced new farm lending criteria, which led to much debate and criticism among farming leaders. Meanwhile, bank customers – now infinitely more assertive than formerly, and less inclined to be loyal on grounds of mere tradition – rightly sensed growing competition. They began to ask more questions, and to shop around.

The obvious competition between the banks, and their growing concern about corporate image, also saw another new phenomenon surface around this time, in the form of the sponsorship proposal. A seemingly never-ending line of people suddenly appeared with suggestions for sponsorships that would supposedly enhance the bank's image while enabling *them* to cover costs or make money. The proponents ranged from those prepared (at a price) to allow the bank to sponsor a Formula One motor-racing car to those offering hoardings for advertising at local sheep-shearing competitions. To keep an element of sanity in this daily round and ensure that we were not being played off against one another, Angela Cotter and I maintained almost daily contact with our friends and counterparts in the Bank of Ireland, Donal O'Donovan and Sean MacQuaid.

Another development in a wider context that occurred around this time was the establishment of an informal group of European public relations managers in banking, which met in a different country every year. Conceived as a forum for the exchange of ideas and information, it was the brainchild of a plump, genial, Swiss gentleman, Bob Peterson, and it thus became known to the participants as 'The Round Peterson Table'. Through it, I learned a lot about the common public relations problems facing banks throughout Europe, made many contacts and friends, and enjoyed the opportunity of visiting European cities previously unknown to me.

~

In the late 1970s, rumours began to surface in Dublin pubs about the Taoiseach, Charles Haughey. From near political oblivion after his dismissal from the Cabinet by the Taoiseach, Jack Lynch, following the Arms Trial in 1970, Haughey had painstakingly worked his way back to power to become leader of Fianna Fáil. As an effective minister and later as Taoiseach, Haughey was responsible for some imaginative legislative measures, among them the removal of income tax for artists and the introduction of free public transport for pensioners. He possessed both the so-called 'common touch' and a certain charisma, but although he inspired total devotion in many, there were always some who viewed him sceptically, even within his own party.

Charles Haughey was generally understood to be a very wealthy man who lived in the grand manner. Gossip suggested a lifestyle that was flamboyant, yet tasteful. He exuded a confidence and sophistication that could hardly have been imagined in Ireland before then, in some ways recalling the landed gentry whom the 'Soldiers of Destiny' had largely dispossessed. He offered a glimpse of their privileged way of life – but this time, as led by 'one of our own'. For many, Haughey exemplified the New Ireland, or at least its possibilities.

The source of Charlie Haughey's wealth had been a topic of general conversation for some time. His income as a politician was modest enough, but his lifestyle was lavish. He was known to be something of a financial wizard, and there was a public perception that he had probably come by his fortune by means of shrewd investments. Some simply put the gossip down to sour grapes. By the end of the 1970s, however, there were journalists who were beginning to show as much interest in Haughey's lifestyle as in his political activities, and this led them back to his bank account in the Dame Street branch of AIB, previously the Munster & Leinster.

In the bank's public relations office, we received at first only a very occasional query in this matter. The response was as it would have been had the subject been any other account-holder: customer information was never divulged. Within the bank, however, it was obvious from the demeanour of some senior executives that a serious problem had arisen, although a discreet veil of silence prevailed.

Much of what was happening is now common knowledge. The bank, despite its deepening concern about Haughey's finances and its many appeals to him to address the problem, was having no success. It continued to honour his cheques, however, and with reason: he was, after all, one of the most powerful men in the country. With its roots in the Munster & Leinster, a long-time supporter of the founders of the state, AIB was not disposed to pull the plug on the leader of Ireland's largest political party.

There were one or two journalists who were especially keen to get to the heart of the Haughey story, and who raised it with me again and again. One of them was Des Crowley, a freelance financial correspondent who looked more like a pirate or a black-bearded fisherman. He had raised the Haughey question before, but one day he phoned me sounding particularly excited, having obviously picked up some information elsewhere. 'Come on, Bob, admit it,' he pressed me good-naturedly. 'It's over a million, isn't it? Come on, you can't deny it!' As I knew no more (and possibly less) than he did, the conversation didn't go far, and not being one to entertain hard feelings, he ended it abruptly and headed off to pursue some other lead. It was an interchange that was to be repeated many times.

I passed Des Crowley's remarks on to the bank executive, but got no authoritative statement that might confirm or deny his story, although I did detect a distinct unease on the fourth floor.

Still foraging, Des Crowley put a report together towards the end of 1982, which he offered to Sean Ward, editor of the Evening Press. It appeared in print on Friday, 28 January, on one of the paper's inside pages, under the headline: *Huge interest in Haughey cashflow*. Given the content of the story, it was a mild headline. It suggested that Haughey, far from being a wealthy man, had been in debt to the bank to the tune of around £1m the previous year. It claimed that 'sources close to the bank' had confirmed the debt, and went on to mention numerous land deals in which it suggested Haughey had been involved.

Not surprisingly, the article led the executive of the bank to enquire of its public relations office if we could throw any light on Crowley's claims. All I could say was that he had been in touch, but that nothing had been confirmed.

In response to the *Evening Press* article, a statement was issued by the bank and published in the paper within days of Des Crowley's article, on 1 February, 1982. It refuted the suggestion that Charles Haughey had owed the bank £1m, describing this as so 'outlandishly inaccurate' that the bank felt compelled to deny it publicly.

I have no recollection of ever having seen this statement other than in the newspaper. It was not until 1999, at the Moriarty Tribunal, that I learned that it was issued on AIB stationery with *Group Public Relations* (or possibly *Group Public Relations Office*) typed at the top. Most unusually, it was undated and unsigned. Furthermore, duplicates had been circulated to some of the bank's senior managers at the time. This was the first time I had ever heard of an AIB press release emanating from anywhere other than the press and public relations office, and releases were always dated, with a contact name and telephone number at the end.

It is true, however, that around this time, AIB was in the process of establishing a new *group* public affairs function, to include Allied Irish Investment Bank and Allied Irish Finance, as well as AIB's blossoming banking operations in the US, Britain and Europe, and its recently acquired interest in the Insurance Corporation of Ireland. The role of the existing public relations office was to become more specifically focused on media relations.

The story in the *Evening Press* appeared when a heave was taking place within Fianna Fáil to remove Haughey from the party leadership. If gone unchallenged, Des Crowley's article could certainly have damaged Haughey and seriously reduced his chances of survival. The bank's statement of denial may well have killed off further questions by other journalists, and it probably helped to secure Haughey's position.

An intriguing question remains. Did he, Charles Haughey (or someone acting on his behalf), make contact with the chairman or chief executive of AIB to request that the bank issue a statement to the press denying the allegations of Des Crowley's story? And who issued the statement?

Haughey survived; the story died. Many years passed before a bizarre event in Florida ultimately led to his financial affairs and his relationship with the bank once again surfacing in the public domain, leading to the creation of the Moriarty Tribunal. A conclusion is unlikely to be reached before this book is published, and I often suspect that we will never have a full answer to the questions raised above, at least not in my lifetime.

~

Another event that occurred around this time which focused public attention on AIB was the collapse of the Insurance Corporation of Ireland. AIB had been expanding rapidly for over a decade and had been on the lookout for opportunities to diversify into other financial markets. The Insurance Corporation of Ireland was the second largest non-life insurer in the state, with a turnover of some £380m and over 800 employees. Seventy per cent of its business lay outside Ireland, mostly in the UK.

AIB first entered the insurance market in December 1981, when it purchased twenty-five per cent of ICI at a cost of £10.2m. The remaining seventy-five per cent of the company was acquired in late 1983 for a further £34.6m. Twenty years ago, these were immense sums, representing a huge investment on the bank's part. The acquisition was seen as a significant strategic move, and in its immediate aftermath an air of hubris seemed to waft about the upper floors of Bankcentre. ICI, meanwhile, was congratulating itself on having secured a powerful new owner.

The first sign of trouble came when pre-tax profits to December 1983 fell from the previous year's £8.2m to £2m. Surely this was not in the original script? ICI made soothing sounds to ease AIB's anxiety about the sudden downturn, but the bank's foreboding only increased when the deterioration in trading performance was compounded by news of ICI's under-provision for reserves, to the tune of £23m, according to an assessment of November 1984. Concern rose among those monitoring the situation both in ICI and in AIB – but who would confront the executive of the bank with the precarious situation that was developing?

Meanwhile, rumours from London about ICI's operations in the City had been openly circulating among journalists for some time. The management of the company there, it seemed, had adopted a free-wheeling style that had given it a reputation for insuring the sort of business that other insurers would not touch with the proverbial bargepole. Its spectacular insurance failures were becoming a talking point among insurance executives in London's cafés and wine bars.

Irish financial journalists were interested in these stories, but their comments and queries to the bank were met with a blank: it was as if hard news of ICI's eccentric activity in London had not yet reached Bankcentre. Despite the losses that had occurred, those at the top in the bank took the line that the rumours were without foundation and that the company was in order.

By November 1984, however, ICI's insurance solvency ratio called for immediate attention, and a rescue operation was needed to forestall the company's collapse. In the hope of resolving the situation, AIB purchased additional shares to a value of £40m. Things continued to deteriorate. A special investigation revealed that potential losses could now reach between £60m and £130m, sums of mammoth proportions in the mid-1980s.

Neither the general public nor the vast majority of the staff of the bank were aware of the seriousness of the situation. ICI had 120,000 insurance policies in Ireland, 30,000 of them in motor insurance. It held twenty-five per cent of the country's employer's liability and public liability insurance business, much of it in the semi-state sector. Without this cover, it would be difficult to sustain employment over wide areas of the economy. Those who were beginning to feel nervous feared that national transport systems could be affected, with planes grounded and trains and buses unable to run. Add to this a possible run on the currency and the collapse of the banking system, and the picture became extremely alarming.

With disaster on the horizon, minds at last became concentrated, and a plan of action was devised. The government and the Central Bank were informed of the seriousness of the situation, as were the other banks and the Dublin and international stock exchanges. The biggest problem was the difficulty in ascertaining the exact extent of the losses at ICI. The mood in Bancentre was sombre.

One of the immediate tasks was to inform the media, and a press briefing was arranged. It turned out to be a memorable one, with the media descending like bloodhounds on a trail. Serious business journalists had to elbow their way through the paparazzi and fight unfamiliar competition to get in first with their questions. Could the bank quantify the loss? When did the disastrous situation in London first come to the bank's notice? Hadn't the dogs in the street known all along what was happening? Who was going to take responsibility? Would anyone resign?

The story broke on the eve of the long St. Patrick's Day weekend, giving the bank time to mobilise its forces. Regional managers conveyed the gravity of the situation to the managers of the branches, in many cases at meetings in their own homes over that weekend. The branch managers would have the daunting task of calming depositors and allaying the anxieties of a nervous public, to help prevent a run on the bank. Meanwhile, back at headquarters, the important task of reassuring the shareholders – the effective owners of the bank – also had to be faced.

The Fine Gael / Labour Coalition Government came under immediate pressure, since the ball was now firmly in their court. The survival of the country's banking system was at stake, with perhaps even the economy itself under threat. There was the possibility of a massive exodus of capital, and international confidence in Ireland would be affected.

To get a sense of the political temperature, I spent some days in the Dáil listening to the debates on the crisis. Despite raised levels of public anxiety, the business of the House moved at its usual sedate pace. In committee rooms and in the Dáil bar, however, events were being vigorously dissected and analysed. Most of the conversations I was party to centred on the pressure on the government to produce a rescue operation, and on what it might expect from AIB in return. A suggestion that came up repeatedly was that the government might take an equity stake in AIB in return for a rescue package, a solution that would have the virtue of simplicity, although the size of the shareholding would depend on the funding required.

In the event, in March 1985 the Insurance Corporation of Ireland was acquired by the state for a nominal sum and placed under the control of the Minister for Industry, Trade, Commerce and Tourism. For its part, AIB agreed to write off its investment of £85m, recognising that it was unlikely to resolve the problems it had inherited without risking damage to the bank and perhaps bringing down the banking system in the process. An administrator was appointed by the government to take over the functions of the board and management of ICI and carry it on as a going concern.

I was surprised that the idea of the government taking a stake in the bank disappeared like snow from a summer ditch without further mention. True, it would hardly have sat comfortably with Fine Gael, but it would have been in line with the Labour Party's philosophy at the time in bringing a financial institution into public ownership. And had the Fianna Fáil opposition, led by Charles Haughey, decided to run with the concept, they could have put pressure on the Labour Party and created strains in the Coalition.

On the other hand, a substantial portion of the pension funds of national organisations, including the trade unions, were invested in bank shares, and any weakening of AIB would have been viewed with alarm. An equity stake by the government in the bank would probably have been regarded by some as setting a dangerous precedent, while in international financial circles (dominated by the US), it would have been seen as socialism through the back door. It brought home to me once again the power of the 'establishment' and the fact that forces far beyond an immediate situation are often central in determining its resolution.

Despite the ICI *débâcle*, AIB's confidence remained undiminished. It quickly dusted itself down, put the collapse of the insurance company behind it, and continued its vigorous expansion, both nationally and internationally. The new management structures conceived by Brian Whelan probably not only helped the bank to recover from the ICI trauma, but also underpinned its further growth.

While the drama at home was unfolding, an important development was well under way across the Atlantic: the purchase by AIB of the First National Bank of Maryland, later to become First Maryland Bankcorp. Jerry Casey, manager of the bank's branch on Fifth Avenue, New York, was appointed to head up the North American operation. Under Casey, regarded by many of his peers as one of the most gifted of the younger generation in AIB, the American bank expanded its activities in a relatively short time not only in Maryland, but also in Virginia, Pennsylvania, Delaware and Washington DC.

Today, owning a successful banking operation in the world's leading economy must rank among AIB's proudest achievements. If a foreign company should ever attempt to acquire the bank, it will not be for its branch network and its offices in Kildysart, Ballydehob or even Dame Street, but for its thriving international business, which now also includes eastern Europe.

CHAPTER 18

CLOSING STATEMENT

Early retirement was introduced in the bank in the 1980s. Before then, the idea of retiring prematurely was simply out of the question. Becoming part of the furniture, bank officials toiled doggedly on year after year, lured by the promise of a pension at sixty-five. When the appointed day at last arrived, they were presented with a clock or a lawnmower, together with a letter of thanks for their loyal service signed on behalf of the chief executive. A few drinks with colleagues, a few slaps on the back, and the daily routine of almost fifty years came to an abrupt end.

For some, retirement demanded an adjustment that did not come easily. Others couldn't wait to get out. Indeed, there were a few, back in the days before it became possible to retire early and still enjoy the benefits of a pension, who were prepared to go to great lengths in order to win their freedom.

There was one man in the bank who, having discovered that the only short cut to retirement was through certified illness, and being cursed with robust good health, decided to have himself declared mentally unstable. He took to talking to himself and coming to work pulling a duck on a lead, which he tied to his chair in the office. When this failed, he came up with a better idea. He would leave his house in the morning dragging a large wooden cross over his shoulder as he headed up the street, muttering and stumbling a few times before hauling it into the bank, where he would prop it against a wall. This did the trick, and he was discreetly retired from service.

It is hard to imagine being this desperate to escape from a job, but by the mid-1980s, my own feet were starting to itch. It was becoming clear to me that public relations, in banking as elsewhere, was moving in a direction with which I no longer felt comfortable. The old definition of public relations as 'the planned and sustained effort to establish and maintain mutual understanding between an organisation and its public' was taking on new meanings. Event management was becoming central. Also, as organisations grew, PR practitioners were turning into mouthpieces for an increasingly anonymous 'management', composed of people they barely knew. Decisions and policies still had to be explained and justified to the public and the media, but the PR official would often know as little about the real reasons behind those decisions as those they were trying to inform.

What had once called for good communications skills, a sense of timing, an ability to think on one's feet if necessary, and above all, a capacity to get on well with all kinds of people, was rapidly turning into a science, with its own textbooks and formulae. Professional consultancies were springing up like mushrooms. Arriving on the national scene were the 'doctors of spin', capable of refining the meaning of language itself, coining pithy phrases and creating appropriate sound-bytes. Public relations was becoming a firefighting operation. I began to think about getting out.

It is rarely easy to pinpoint the exact moment at which such an idea takes root. Often, there *is* none: it is like a seed carried in the wind and dropped unnoticed on the ground, where it sprouts and slowly begins to grow.

It was around this time that I became interested in the old Irish custom of 'hunting the wran' on St. Stephen's Day. For years I had been aware that many of these old traditions, once practised widely around the country, were dying out. 'The Wran' involved scores of young men disguised with blackened faces, who would go from house to house on 26 December, singing, playing music and terrifying people into parting with a few pennies. Originally, the money was supposed to go towards the cost of burying a wren that was hunted down and killed beforehand, which was carried around by the Wran Boys as they chanted their traditional rhymes. In practice, it was used to buy drink. The slaughter of the harmless bird had been eliminated many years ago, but the singing and dressing up was still practised in just a few areas.

One day among friends I had suggested trying to rekindle this pre-Christian revelry in Dublin, and before you could say 'Con Howard', a committee had been formed. Over a hundred heavily disguised Wran 'boys' and 'girls' turned out for the event which took place in Ranelagh on St. Stephen's morning. They danced behind a tractor pulling a float on which one of the Chieftains beat out a lively rhythm on a bodhran, leading them like the Pied Piper of Hamelin through the sleepy streets. Rory O'Conor ('the

O'Conor Don'), descendent of the last High King of Ireland, accompanied by the Australian ambassador and the ubiquitous Con Howard, rode in a horse-drawn coach. Behind them came a mixed bag of ordinary citizens – including my long-suffering family – and familiar faces from the worlds of business, the judiciary, politics, the media and entertainment. They included Ruaraí Quinn (present leader of the Labour Party); Paddy Moriarty, then chief executive of the ESB; Irish traditional singer, Dolly McMahon, and her husband, the broadcaster, Ciáran MacMathúna, perhaps best known for his invaluable audio archive of Irish music and song.

One prominent figure, completely unknown to me, threw himself into the proceedings with enthusiasm, his boot-polished face exuding mischief and *joie-de-vivre*. He turned out to be Tom Ahern, who worked in Kevin Street College and had travelled from Co. Kildare for the occasion, having read about it in the newspaper. I later discovered that Tom also seemed to fulfil the unofficial function of cultural attaché to the college. I had made a new friend.

Perhaps partly because St. Stephen's Day is one of those days when the media are hungry for a story that is both newsworthy and light-hearted, the Wran received wide coverage. I was surprised to open the *Irish Times* the following day and see a photo of myself with blackened face and fancy dress on the front page, and we even featured on the RTE news.

Back at the bank after Christmas, I was greeted good-humouredly by many about my new role as a Wran Boy – although I must confess to having a fleeting moment of wondering how the picture in the *Irish Times* might sit with the image the bank was then actively promoting. However, a genuine attempt to revive an old custom had proved successful and enjoyable for everyone, and it had also raised money for the Hospice, both of which had given me real satisfaction. I found myself thinking again about the feasibility of moving on to explore avenues outside the bank, perhaps closer to my natural sympathies.

Central to quitting one's job, however, is the question of money. The American writer, Damon Runyon, once famously remarked, 'Always try to rub up against money, for [if you do] some of it may rub off on you'. Clearly, he never worked in a bank. In all my years in banking, I had rarely if ever seen anyone become rich, and certainly not in my own circle. At this time, I was still only in my mid-fifties, and some of my family were still in full-time education. If I were to leave the bank, I would have to find an alternative source of income.

A plan began to form. In a way, it was one that went back many years. I have already described some of the methods devised by Irish bankers to support themselves and their families during the two long bank strikes of 1966 and 1970. It was during the first of these, in 1966, that I had first had the opportunity to put to the test a notion I had harboured for years as little more than a wild dream. Could I earn a living by painting?

After the early exhibitions with Tony O'Malley and Jimmy Manning in the late 1950s, I had shared two further exhibitions with Jimmy in 1961 and 1962. I had exhibited with the Royal Hibernian Academy and at an exhibition of Irish sacred art, and I had participated in group shows as well as having two of my own. I had sold quite a few paintings, so I had established that there were people willing to pay for them.

One thing was certain: creative visions were all very well, but reality dictated that anything too highfalutin' would not put bread on the table. By the mid-1960s, however, tourism was really taking off, and it occurred to me that there might be a market for miniature landscapes among the coachloads of American visitors driving around the country. I had in mind something along the lines of Paul Henry or Maurice MacGonigal, or the brooding pastoral scenes of Nathaniel Hone, but at prices affordable to tourists. Any reservations I might have had about 'selling my soul' were quickly put aside in favour of more immediate practical concerns.

Mary had a full-time job looking after our three lively boys, but she was enthusiastic about the idea and jumped at the opportunity to become involved. She had a far more practical turn of mind than I ever had, and we had many debates about how best to approach the venture. Pricing was a delicate issue, pragmatically tied in with size rather than artistic merit. Frames were expensive, and Americans were known to be keen on value for their dollar. Furthermore, the pictures would have to fit easily into hand luggage. We eventually decided that the unframed paintings would have to measure seven inches by four. As for pricing, when Tony, Jimmy and I had exhibited some five years previously, we had daringly charged at figures ranging from five to ten pounds. The miniatures would have to cost substantially less than five pounds, I decided, and we eventually settled on a guinea, the equivalent in pre-decimal currency of one pound and one shilling. (I have not yet come to grips with the Euro.)

As the business would be launched with a serious deficit of capital, canvas or proper art paper was far too expensive to be considered. Instead, I laboriously cut strips of hardboard into the appropriate shape and size, and covered them with a preparatory undercoat of 'size', otherwise known as glue. This done, a painting frenzy overtook me, and bogs, mountains, rivers, lakes, trees and haystacks appeared as if by magic. At the end of the first day, I looked around and assessed my handiwork. So far, so good.

The next problem was framing, and Jimmy Manning pointed me in the direction of a Jewish framer, Mr. Marcus, who had a business in the aromatic territory adjoining O'Keeffe's ('the knacker's yard') between Cork Street and the Coombe. O'Keeffe's speciality was turning dead donkeys and horses into glue, probably the very glue I had used in producing my pictures. I had cycled past it regularly during my Dame Street years, pressing hard on the pedals and holding my breath to avoid inhaling the fumes.

My first visit to Marcus was a journey to another world. Dressed in brown overalls, he worked in rickety premises surrounded on all sides by religious iconography, images of the Sacred Heart and Virgin Mary jostling with Padre Pios and assorted saints and martyrs. I had arrived at the epicentre of Ireland's holy picture industry, and from the piles stacked against the walls, business was brisk.

I showed Mr. Marcus a sample of the paintings I had completed, hinting that my initial requirement might be followed by substantial repeat orders. Marcus was an astute man. He listened to my story sympathetically, with a twinkle in his eye. After a few minutes haggling (a skill I never really mastered), a deal was struck: a simple unvarnished wooden frame would cost half-a-crown; a slightly larger, painted version was five shillings and ninepence. I decided that our need would be mostly for the cheaper ones. We were in business.

The framed paintings looked good, but we still faced the challenge of selling them. Nothing daunted, Mary set out for town, optimistically bearing an order book along with a dozen framed pictures in an attaché case. As she stepped off the bus at St. Stephen's Green, her eye fell on *Maison Prost*, a high-class hairdressing salon which also had a small retail area selling expensive cosmetics and a limited range of exclusive giftware. Showing great initiative, she entered, introduced herself to Mrs. Prost and displayed her wares. Probably as impressed with my director of marketing as with the paintings, Mrs. Prost promptly bought the lot – before launching into a verbal attack on the striking bankers and the trouble they were causing her, while Mary struggled to sound sympathetic and keep a straight face.

It was a good start. Mary had discovered a hidden talent, and within weeks the pictures were on sale in Brown Thomas' and the Hibernian Hotel. Aer Rianta displayed them in showcases at Dublin, Shannon and Cork airports, while Switzers, Avoca Handweavers, the Intercontinental Hotel and other outlets ordered them by the dozen. Selling at a guinea each, they left us with a gross profit of about ten shillings, or fifty new pence.

As Mary returned to Dundrum each evening with another full order book, the whirlwind of activity intensified in an upstairs room. Drying the paint quickly became a problem. Acrylic paint had yet to become available, and the work was being marketed as original oil paintings. One evening, Mary – who was only getting into her stride – got back from her day's labours and almost provoked an unofficial stoppage in the workshop by announcing that she had secured a large order from Pan-American Airways. In two weeks' time, they would be flying 250 American VIPs into Ireland, and they would like to present each of them with a gift of an Irish landscape painting. Could we fulfil the order in time?

Things were getting out of hand. A new method of production was urgently needed, and after some frantic head-scratching, I eventually came up with a solution. I set out for the local hardware shop and returned with some long strips of hardboard measuring twelve feet by four inches. Perspiring heavily, I manoeuvred them, wobbling dangerously, up the stairs to the spare bedroom, and stacked them against a wall. I took the first and balanced it carefully between a chair and the foot of the bed. Then, rolling up my sleeves and seizing my brush, I threw myself into an orgy of painting. Across the upper half of the board, cerulean and cobalt blue fused with titanium white and magenta to become a wild, billowing (twelve-foot-long) sky. Beneath this, viridian, sap and olive green snaked through swathes of cadmium yellow spliced with burnt sienna, raw ochre and light grey. The result was a moody landscape. In its finished state I thought it looked more than acceptable, even if a little eccentric in its proportions, stretching, as it did, from one end of the room to the other, while still measuring only four inches high.

The second stage of the operation demanded concentration. Moving along the board, I very carefully measured and marked out seven-inch sections. A trip to the garden shed followed, and with a bit of rummaging around, I eventually located the saw. Some more perspiration, a few near-misses with my thumb, and hey, presto! – I had twenty paintings ready for framing.

It took thirteen strips of hardboard and three days' work to complete the Pan-Am order. The hair-dryer was pressed into service to help dry the paint. When the paintings were finished, I looked at them and scratched my head: they looked equal to if not better than the earlier, more laboured work. It was as if having that long sweep of empty space to work in was somehow liberating, while the challenge of the shallow depth somehow made the task more interesting. Would that the strike might last!

It didn't. Within months, I was back at work in the bank, and the idea of earning a living by painting was shelved away again. The years passed. Throughout the decades described in these pages I continued to paint. It was somehow typical that I did so in spurts, intervals of energy and inspiration alternating with periods when my interest was absorbed elsewhere.

By the mid-1980s, I had had a total of eleven one-man shows in galleries in Dublin and Cork, as well as one in Annapolis, in Maryland, USA. Almost twenty years after that first venture into the world of commerce, thoughts of full-time painting began to surface again. Was there a future beyond banking? I was ready for a change, and I began to talk it over with friends whose opinions I respected, especially Brian McCarthy and Pat O'Mahony, then head of marketing in the bank and later general manager, Branches & Technology. Most of all, I discussed it with Mary, and we debated my prospects and the needs of the family at length. Naturally, the biggest issue was what a dramatic drop in income might mean, but when we had weighed up all the pros and cons together, Mary generously left the final decision to me.

I have never been one to delay for long at a crossroads.

Shortly after my fifty-fifth birthday, after nearly forty years in the bank (seventeen of them in PR), I bade farewell to a life I had been born into. Retiring from the bank was like leaving a kind of priesthood, with its own peculiar hierarchy and commandments, rites and rituals. It was one to which I could hardly have been less suited by nature, but expectations about job satisfaction and personal fulfilment through work did not weigh heavily on my generation, and I cannot honestly say that I ever lost much sleep wondering if my life might have been better or more useful if I had applied any abilities I might have to something else.

My plan to paint for a living did not work out quite as expected. Having decided that my days behind a desk were finished for good (I had always managed to keep them to a minimum in any case), I somehow found myself doing some PR consultancy work in the months immediately after retirement.

My sons had built me a fine studio at the bottom of our garden, but once again fate seemed determined to thwart my ambition to become a full-time artist. This time it came in the shape of a phone-call from Bill Ambrose, part-owner and managing editor of *Business & Finance* magazine. He had a plan, he said, to revive *Dublin Opinion*, the satirical humorous magazine originally founded in the 1920s which had flourished in Ireland for the best part of four decades. Would I consider becoming its editor? I could hardly have been more surprised. My first reaction was to express serious doubts that I was qualified for the job, but the finality of 'no' as an answer to most things has always struck me as dull, especially when measured against the possibilities implied in a 'yes', so I accepted.

Unfortunately, *Dublin Opinion* failed to capture the market (and particularly the advertising revenue) needed to survive. Two years later, equally unpredictably, I found myself once again in full-time employment, this time as marketing director with the registered charity, *Cerebral Palsy Ireland*. Both of these experiences brought interesting new acquaintances, fresh adventures, new friends, much laughter and more stories to tell.

I suppose I could say that I finally retired in 1997, with, in theory at least, unlimited time to paint at last (there are days when nine small representatives of a new generation of Ryans seem to keep me fairly busy with chauffeuring duties, having already managed, in the space of a few short years, to undermine my image of *boulevardier* and replace it with the rather less exalted one of *dandan*).

As regards painting, what have I produced? There has been one period of intense activity, inspired by a visit to Spain in 1993. Apart from that, very little. Instead, I have somehow found myself huddled at strange hours of the night and day over a computer, using two index fingers and a mind that has always resisted the concept of 'order' to try and put form, sequence and coherence on the tumble of recollections, observations and anecdotes that are the legacy of almost forty years in banking.

Ordinary bankers rarely make front-page news. Like accountants and civil servants, they are often painted in drab colours, but that is not how I remember the people I worked with, or the many others I came to know through my job in the bank. To me, they were truly 'the salt of the earth'. In them I found the full spectrum of the best (and very occasionally the worst!) of human qualities and attributes. Through them, I found as much stimulation, amusement, entertainment and satisfaction as anyone could ever hope to experience in a working life. These pages have aimed, in a small way, to pay homage to them all – including those who are no longer mentioned, now that my original draft has been reluctantly pruned back to half its original length. I hope that no one will take offence at what at all times have been intended as affectionate tributes.

Almost fifteen years after retiring from the bank, I still cherish the memories.

Now...where's that paint-brush?